NEW CLAiT 2006

in
easy steps

In easy steps is an imprint of Computer Step
Southfield Road · Southam
Warwickshire CV47 0FB · United Kingdom
www.ineasysteps.com

This edition is endorsed by OCR for use with the
New CLAiT 2006 specification

Notice of Liability
Every effort has been made to ensure that this book contains accurate and
current information. However, Computer Step and the author shall not be
liable for any loss or damage suffered by readers as a result of any information
contained herein.

Trademarks
Microsoft® and Windows® are registered trademarks of Microsoft
Corporation. All other trademarks are acknowledged as belonging to their
respective companies.

Printed and bound in the United Kingdom

ISBN-13 978-1-84078-309-4
ISBN-10 1-84078-309-5

Table of Contents

File Management and e-Document Production	9
Your computer	10
The software	12
Your workstation	13
Starting the computer	14
The Start menu and Taskbar	16
A standard window	17
Exploring files and folders	18
Navigate the folders	20
Folder commands	21
Manage files	22
Identify files	24
Word processing	25
Optimise your view	27
Page layout	29
Enter text	30
Editing text	31
The Spell Checker	33
Save your document	34
Close the file and program	36
Open an existing file	37
Select text	38
Format text	39
Alignment and line spacing	40
Move and copy text	41
Find and replace	43
Headers and footers	44
Tables	45
Tabs and indents	47
Bullets and numbering	48
Print preview	49
Print your file	50
Your printer	51

Managing the printer   52
Print folder contents   53
Shutdown   54
Unit 1 exercise   55

Creating Spreadsheets and Graphs   59

The spreadsheet   60
Create a spreadsheet   62
Change the layout   63
Sort   66
Creating formulae   67
Functions   68
The Fill tool   72
Copying formulae   73
Numeric format   75
Text format   76
Borders and shading   77
Headers and footers   78
Printing spreadsheets   80
Charts   82
Parts of a chart   83
Create a pie chart   84
Bar/column chart   88
Line graph   89
Editing charts   90
The chart toolbar   91
Amend the scale   92
Troubleshooting   93
Changing segment display   95
Printing charts   96
Unit 2 exercise   97

Database Manipulation 101

The database 102
Start Access 103
The main database window 104
Tables 105
Editing the table 107
Find and replace 108
Sort 109
Filters 110
Queries 111
Create a query 112
Printing tables and queries 114
Reports 115
Close the database 119
Create your own table 120
Unit 3 exercise 122

e-Publication Creation 125

Desktop publishing 126
Start Publisher 127
The Publisher window 128
Create a page layout 129
Templates 130
Frames and boxes 131
Import text 134
Overflow text 135
Fonts 136
Text alignment 137
Import an image file 138
Image management 139
Drawing tools 140

Borders   141
Final publication layout   142
Printing publications   143
Unit 4 exercise   144

Create an e-Presentation   147

5

Presentation graphics   148
Slide layouts   149
The Slide Master   150
Slide Master text   152
Insert an image   153
Applying a slide layout   154
Bulleted text   155
Text tools   156
Autoshapes   157
Arranging slides   158
Printing   159
The Slide Show   161
Unit 5 exercise   162

e-Image Creation   165

6

Computer art   166
The software   168
Using Paint Shop Pro   170
Create the canvas   171
Load and insert image   172
Resize image   173
Resize and Crop   174
Vector layers   175
Draw preset shape   176
Enter text   177

Edit artwork   178
Transfer digital photographs   180
Change image resolution   182
Print image   183
Unit 6 exercise   185

Web Page Creation   189

HTML Editors and Browsers   190
FrontPage   192
Build the web   194
Open web pages   196
Create links   197
Save, Close, Reopen   198
Create a new web page   199
Format the page   200
Insert an image   202
Insert external links   203
Check the links   204
View in browser   206
Hyperlinks view   207
Printing web page and HTML   208
Publish your web   209
Unit 7 exercise   210

Online Communication   213

E-mail and the Internet   214
Internet security   216
Viruses   217
Start Outlook Express   218
Receive e-mail   220
The Address Book   221

Receive attachments   223
Create e-mail   225
Send, reply and forward   227
Send an attachment   230
Organise your mail   231
Print your e-mail   232
The World Wide Web   233
Search engines   235
Save images and text   238
Manage web addresses   240
Printing web pages   241
Unit 8 exercise   242

IC³, Webwise and Downloads   245

The IC³ Exams   246
IC³ Exam Demo   247
IC³ Exam Objectives   248
BBC Webwise   251
Download files   253
Where next?   255

Index   257

File Management and e-Document Production

This unit is mandatory for the New CLAiT 2006 qualification. The chapter introduces essential terminology and tasks which are common to all units such as creating and navigating folders, managing files and using the printer. The unit itself covers fundamental word processing techniques, including creating, saving and printing documents, editing and formatting.

Covers

Your computer | 10

Starting the computer | 14

Exploring files and folders | 18

Word processing | 25

Enter and edit text | 30

The Spell checker | 33

Save and close | 34

Working with text | 38

Alignment and spacing | 40

Move and copy text | 41

Headers and footers | 44

Tables | 45

Tabs and indents | 47

Bullets and numbering | 48

Print preview and printing | 49

Shutdown | 54

Unit 1 exercise | 55

Unit One

Your computer

Your computer may look like the one illustrated, with many separate pieces of hardware, or it may be as compact as a laptop, but it should fundamentally consist of the same elements.

The systems unit

The disk drives on your computer are referred to by a letter followed by a colon. The hard disk inside the systems unit is usually known as the C: drive, and the floppy disk as the A: drive.

This is where the disk drives, memory chips and adapter cards are located. The main hard disk is the storage area for programs that are loaded onto your computer. Its size or capacity for storage is measured in gigabytes (approximately one thousand million bytes). The unit may also contain the floppy drive, a CD drive and perhaps a DVD drive.

The memory is where the activity takes place on the computer. When you create or change a document the information is held in memory until you save it to disk. The memory chips are measured in megabytes (approximately one million bytes).

The adapter cards allow you to attach hardware, such as a monitor, keyboard, mouse and printer.

A resolution of 800 by 600 will give you larger text and icons on your monitor, but the detail will not be as fine.

The monitor

The monitor has two measurements – the actual physical size which is expressed in inches or centimetres, and the resolution which is measured in pixels (picture elements). Most monitors use a resolution of 1024 by 768. The number of colours you can use is 256, 64 thousand (16 bit) or 16 million (32 bit).

...cont'd

The function key, F1, takes you to Help in most programs.

In computing, a space is treated as a character. Use the right arrow, not the spacebar, to move the cursor to the right.

The arrow keys, Home, End, Page Up and Page Down allow you to move around your document.

Single click the mouse to select an item, double click the item to apply an action such as Open.

If you are left-handed you can exchange the actions. Select Start, Settings, Control Panel, Mouse.

The keyboard

There are many different styles of keyboard – standard, ergonomically designed, ones with built-in wrist rests and even some with programmable keys. It is worth studying the keyboard before you switch the computer on.

The standard keyboard has 105 keys. You will see the normal qwerty keys in the central section with number keys above. Below the letters is the spacebar. To the left and right of the letters are the shift keys, indicated by an arrow on each pointing forwards. You must press and hold the shift key to get the symbols on the number keys. Also press the shift key to get a single capital letter. The Caps Lock key is for a series of capitals. The large key to the right of the letters is the Enter or Carriage Return key.

Escape Key   Shift Key

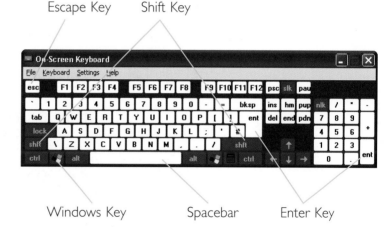

Windows Key   Spacebar   Enter Key

On the right is the number keypad, with its own set of mathematical symbols (+-*/) and Enter key. To get numbers the Num Lock light must be on.

The mouse

There are mice with two buttons, three buttons or scrolling wheels. The first or left mouse button is used as Enter or to select an item. Mouse button two or the right button presents different menus depending on which item is selected. The function of the third or centre button also varies. If you have a three button mouse check the manual to see what other functions are available – you may need to install additional software to enable them.

The software

The operating system

The most important piece of software on your computer is the operating system. This is the program that allows you to use the keyboard, disk drives, monitor etc. It also allows you to use other programs such as the word processor.

There are several operating systems including Windows, Apple Mac and Unix. In this book we are using Windows XP. If your operating system software is a different version of Windows (other than Windows 3.x), you will still be able to use this book, as there are few differences between the versions at the New CLAiT 2006 level of use.

Microsoft Office

Microsoft sells Office in versions which do not have all the programs – you may find, for example, that Access in not included in your copy of Office.

In this book we are using the Office XP Professional package which provides the full range of software required to complete all the New CLAiT 2006 units.

You should be able to follow the illustrations and guides, even if you have a different release of Office, as the methods to complete the activities required by New CLAiT 2006 are almost identical in all releases.

The following list identifies each unit with the appropriate Office program:

● Unit 1	File Management and e-Document Production	Windows and Word
● Unit 2	Creating Spreadsheets and Graphs	Excel
● Unit 3	Database Manipulation	Access
● Unit 4	e-Publication Creation	Publisher
● Unit 5	Create an e-Presentation	PowerPoint
● Unit 6	e-Image Creation	Word
● Unit 7	Web Page Creation	FrontPage
● Unit 8	Online Communication	Outlook Express Internet Explorer

Your workstation

Your computer and its surrounding equipment, such as printer, desk, chair and telephone is known as your workstation. You should design the layout of your workstation so that you sit correctly and can reach most of the equipment easily, without undue strain or stretching.

Repetitive Strain Injury (RSI) can be caused by sitting incorrectly at your computer.

1   The correct sitting position is with your thighs parallel to the floor and your feet flat on the floor or on a foot rest. If you cannot adjust your chair, use a cushion. Your back should be straight and well supported. Your arms should be relaxed and hang straight from the shoulder, with your forearms parallel to the floor and your wrists straight, not bent awkwardly.

2   The keyboard should be adjustable and at a comfortable height. The mouse should be near the keyboard and easy to reach.

3   The monitor should be at the proper viewing distance, between 18 and 24 inches away, directly in front of you rather than at an angle. The height should be adjusted so that you can look slightly down at it. It should also be at right angles to the window or light source to avoid glare.

Document or copy stands are very useful. They should be positioned close to the monitor and at the same height.

4   You should take short breaks to prevent muscle fatigue, get up once in a while and walk around. Look away from the monitor from time to time to relax your eyes.

Starting the computer

You will need to switch on the systems unit and possibly the monitor. Some monitors are powered through the systems unit, and some are independently powered. It is worth turning on the monitor first, as you will be able to read any information and error messages as the computer starts up.

As the computer starts, it goes through a process called the Power On Self Test (POST). It will check its memory and the hardware attached – you may see the keyboard lights flash, and hear the printer reset. Make sure that there is no floppy data disk in the drive when you start up, since this will interfere with the start up process. If you do leave a disk in the drive by mistake, just follow the instructions to remove the disk and press any key to continue.

The password

The New CLAiT 2006 course requires that you are able to use a password to logon and access a data file. The logon and password may be required as the computer starts, as illustrated here, or it may be required to access a particular file. For security reasons, when you type in your password it will be disguised as a series of asterisks or dots. The question mark allows you to view a password hint. You can create a password hint when you set the password.

It is also possible to set passwords on individual files. In Word, select Tools, Options and the Security tab. Specify a password and click OK.

To begin, click your user name

Michael

Sue
Type your password

The hourglass symbol lets you know that the computer is busy.

Once the ID and password have been accepted, the operating system will continue to load. The Windows desktop screen will appear with a series of pictures or icons on the left side of the monitor. You must wait until the hourglass symbol disappears and becomes an arrow before you can begin to work.

The Desktop

Once the operating system is fully loaded, you will see the desktop. The standard desktop has icons (graphical representations) down the left side of the screen. At the bottom is the Taskbar, with the Start button, Quick Launch bar, and to the right is the System tray.

The Icons

My Computer gives you a view of the hardware and software that is installed on your PC.

My Documents takes you to the folder where data files are stored.

Recycle Bin is where you put files you wish to delete.

To see total capacity, used space and free space on your C: drive, double click My Computer, then single click the C: drive. Click with the right mouse button on the drive icon and from the menu, select Properties.

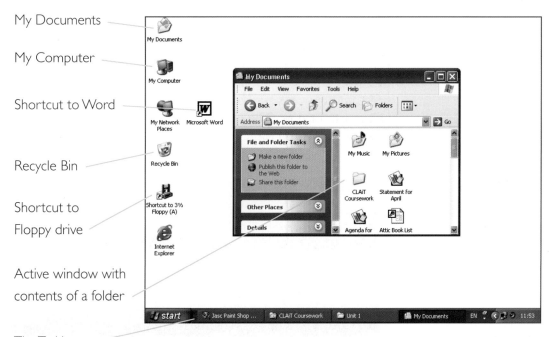

My Documents

My Computer

Shortcut to Word

Recycle Bin

Shortcut to Floppy drive

Active window with contents of a folder

The Taskbar

Internet Explorer can be used as the Internet browser, although you may decide to use an alternative.

There are other standard icons, for example My Network Places. Icons may appear when you install new hardware or software and you can create shortcut icons for yourself which will take you directly to an application, data file or hardware item.

The Start menu and Taskbar

The Start Menu

Click the Start button with the left mouse button. This is the standard way to start using the computer. It gives you access to programs, documents and utilities such as searching for a file.

Programs that you use frequently will be listed above the Start button. For other programs, hover the mouse over All programs and the next level of menu will appear. Move the mouse across and up to the application you want. Then click again.

Selecting My Documents from the Start menu opens the My Documents folder. You can then double click on an existing file to open it.

You may find that the Taskbar is positioned at the top or side of the screen. Click and hold the mouse arrow on a clear section. You can then drag and drop it to which ever edge you prefer.

The Taskbar

The Quick Launch bar opens the application selected. Hover the mouse over the icons to view the purpose of each.

The Notification area is sometimes referred to as the System Tray.

Any applications which are currently running will show on the Taskbar. The active application or window will appear indented (see page 15). As the Taskbar fills, the buttons shrink. Click the program name to see a list of files open in that application.

Hover the mouse over the time to see the date.

The Notification area on the right of the Taskbar shows the time, and utilities such as the virus checker and Internet connection status.

A standard window

The same basic elements comprise a window, whether it is a folder window, or a program window.

If you cannot see the toolbar, select View, Toolbars, Standard Buttons.

These buttons allow you to expand and contract the frame to see more options.

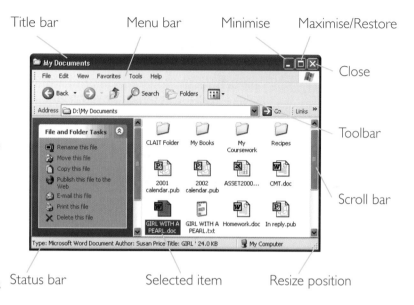

Title bar   Menu bar   Minimise   Maximise/Restore   Close   Toolbar   Scroll bar

Status bar   Selected item   Resize position

To move a window, click and drag the Title bar.

The bright blue Title bar indicates that it is the active window. If the Title bar is pale blue, click in the window to reactivate it.

The Menu bar contains the full list of options for this window.

Most, but not all, windows can be resized. Position the mouse over the edge of the window. When you get the double-headed arrow, you can click and drag.

The blue pane on the left provides access to file and folder tasks, such as copying and deleting files. It also provides details on the selected item, as does the Status bar if visible.

The Toolbar allows you to navigate the folders. Some of the buttons have tips, revealed if you hover the mouse over them.

The Scroll bars only appear when there is too much information to fit the size of the window. Click the arrows at each end of the scroll bar, or hold and drag the sliding bar.

The minimise button shrinks the window but leaves it available on the Taskbar. The Maximise/Restore button toggles between full screen and window. The Close button closes the current window. If it is an application window, the program will check if you wish to save any previously unsaved data.

Exploring files and folders

At the start of Unit 1 you will be supplied with files needed to complete an exercise. You will need to locate those files and follow the instructions to create folders and subfolders, copy files into the folders and subfolders, and move and delete both folders and files.

Windows Explorer is the program to use for managing folders and files on your PC. It shows the organisation of folders in a tree-like structure. It allows you to create, move and delete folders, and to copy, move and delete files.

1 To use Windows Explorer select Start, All Programs, Accessories, Windows Explorer.

> Windows Explorer

2 The window that opens will be divided into two panes. The left pane shows the overall organisation of the drives and folders on the hard disk. The right pane shows folders and files stored within the location selected in the left pane, in this case the main C: drive.

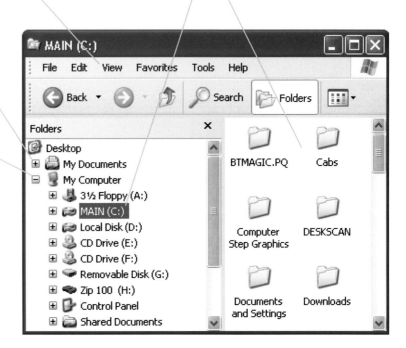

As an alternative to using Explorer, you can double click My Computer on the Desktop.

The window will show the main drives and folders. The left pane shows the Task pane, a Windows XP feature. Double click the main C: drive to view the contents.

2 Click on the Folders icon to see the Folders pane. Click again, or select the close button to return to the System Tasks pane. When you select the Folders icon, the window will look the same as shown in the Explorer window on the opposite page.

Navigate the folders

In Explorer it is easy to move from one folder to another and to view the contents of each. Select the drive or folder in the left pane, and its contents will be displayed in the right pane.

You can also navigate the folders by using the Standard toolbar.

It is possible to move (drag and drop) folders in Explorer inadvertently, so be careful with the mouse.

Double click on a folder in the right-hand pane to open it, or single click and press the Enter key.

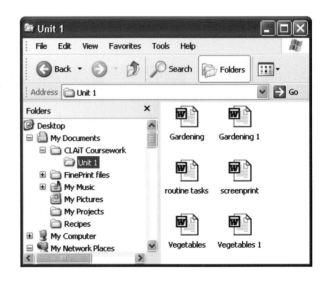

Microsoft Office applications, such as Word and Excel, usually save data files into the My Documents folder.

| The Back and Forward buttons allow you to retrace your steps quickly. You can also select from a list of previous folders.

Select View, Standard toolbar (if it is not already enabled).

2 The Up button opens the parent folder.

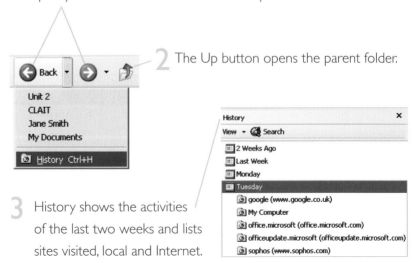

3 History shows the activities of the last two weeks and lists sites visited, local and Internet.

Folder commands

Folders, with their contents, can be copied and moved using the same commands and in the same way as files. See page 22-23 for more details.

1   To create a folder, open Windows Explorer. Select the drive and folder in which to make your new folder. Note that the Title bar shows the name of the selected folder.

2   From the Menu, select File, New, Folder.

When you use the Open file, or Save file function in an application such as Word, you will see the new folder listed.

3   The folder will appear with the New Folder name, highlighted in blue. Simply type the required folder name and press Enter.

You cannot rename or delete a folder if you have it open, or a file within it open.

4   To rename the folder, make sure it is selected. Then click with the right mouse button and select Rename.

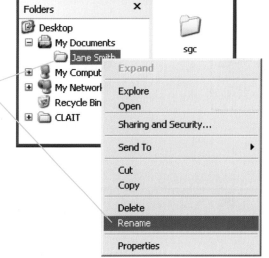

You can delete a folder using the Delete key on the keyboard.

5   To delete the folder, select Delete. The folder and its contents will be removed to the Recycle Bin.

Manage files

Selecting files

1 Open Windows Explorer. In the left pane select, and open if necessary, the folder that contains the required file or files.

2 For a single file, just click on the file in the right pane. You may need to scroll the window to see the file.

3 For a list of adjacent files, select the first in the list, hold down the Shift key and select the last in the list. For randomly spaced files, hold down the Ctrl key as you select, click again to deselect.

For multiple files it's a good idea to switch to the List view in Explorer, as illustrated here, or Details view, as this allows you to see more files at one time.

Use the Shift key to select a block of files

Use the Ctrl key to select individual files

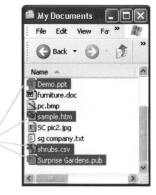

Select View, Toolbars, Customise to add the Cut, Copy and Paste buttons to the Explorer toolbar. You can then use these shortcuts instead of the menu.

Copying files

Windows offers various ways to copy files. Each method has its advantages, but for copying multiple files it is easiest to use the method below.

1 With the file(s) selected, click on Edit, Copy from the Menu.

2 In the left pane of the Explorer window, locate and select the destination folder and select Edit Paste.

If you drag and drop files or folders on the same drive, they will be moved, not copied.

If you make a mistake, or something unexpected happens, you can select Edit, Undo move/copy.

To copy files between different drives, for example A: drive to C: drive, you can use drag and drop. This method is best used for copying one object such as a single file or a complete folder.

3 Select the file in the right pane. Move the cursor with the attached file until the desired location is highlighted in the left (folder) pane. Then release the mouse button. Always check to see that the action has completed successfully.

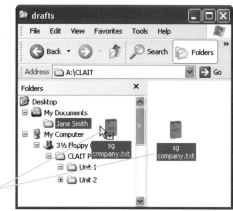

Moving files

| With the files selected, click on Edit, Cut. The files will remain but the icons will appear lighter.

Use the drag and drop method to move files between folders on the same drive.

2 In the left pane of the Explorer window, select the destination folder and click on Edit, Paste.

Deleting files

| With the files selected, just press the Delete key on the keyboard. You will get a message confirming that you wish to delete the file. Files on the C: drive or other hard drive will be moved to the Recycle Bin. If you decide to delete files on the A: drive (floppy disk drive), they will be completely removed, not passed to the recycle bin..

Identify files

You will be given source or data files for the units you decide to take for the course. The files will be different types, appropriate to the data they contain, and for use with specific types of software. Most data file types are associated with a particular program. Part of the installation process for software involves telling Windows which file types use the application. When you double click on a file in Windows Explorer, Windows recognises the association and opens the file in the correct software. Windows provides various ways to identify file types.

furniture.doc	Word
sg company.txt	Text
centre sales.xls	Excel
shrubs.csv	Excel/Access
Attic Book List.mdb	Access
Surprise Gardens.pub	Publisher
Demo.ppt	PowerPoint
sample.htm	FrontPage
SC pic2.jpg	Image
boat.gif	Image
pc.bmp	Paint

On the left are the standard file icons that would be shown in the right hand pane of the Explorer window. In most cases the icon identifies the file type.

For applications such as Word, Excel, PowerPoint etc. the data file type has a standard association. Plain text and image files will open in different programs, according to the way your software is installed.

You can change the way files are shown in the Explorer window, to give more information about the files.

Select View from the Menu bar, or click the down arrow on the Views button

- Thumbnails will show miniature versions of any image files in the folder. This is very useful for folders containing photographs.

- List is best used to display the contents of folders that contain a large number of files. This lets you see the maximum possible.

- Details indicates the file size, type, date and time of modification, especially helpful when you are trying to locate a particular file.

Word processing

Choosing a word processor

In the Windows environment we have access to three types of word processors – NotePad, WordPad and Word. Each program allows us to input and manipulate text, but they do have different roles and capabilities. Notepad is a plain text editor which allows us to move and copy text, but otherwise has limited function. Notepad is useful because the text has no formatting and can be used by almost any application.

Microsoft Word, on the other hand, formats text so that its files can only be read in applications that understand the Word file format, in particular the Office suite of programs. If you wish to transfer the text to other applications, you may need to strip out any formatting, and save it as a text file.

We need to use a full word processor, such as Word, for the New CLAiT 2006 course as we are required to use formatting to emphasise and align text, set margins and manage the document layout. It also provides tools, such as the word count and spell check programs, to ensure that we complete the task successfully.

Word makes formatting text easy as it actually shows us how the text will appear on the page. It is known as a WYSIWYG program – What You See Is What You Get, allowing us to evaluate the formatting and layout. When working through the New CLAiT 2006 exercises, we can check that we have met the requirements.

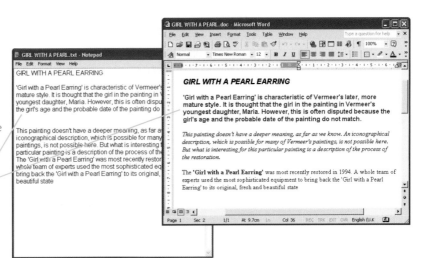

You only need to click the mouse on the Start button, and on the Microsoft Word entry.

Press Start, All Programs, Microsoft Word. This displays the main Word window, showing a blank document screen, ready for you to start typing.

Parts of the Word window:

Menu bar   Title bar   Word's Help facilities

Standard toolbar   Formatting toolbar   Task Pane

See page 37 to open an existing file.

Take note of the names of the various bars, such as Standard toolbar and Status bar as they will be frequently referred to throughout the unit.

Views bar   Cursor location   Status bar   Go to Page bar

If you want to start a second document, click the New Blank Document button on the toolbar. The Title bar will now show Document2. You can have several documents open at once.

The standard Word window gives us a great deal of information. As you become familiar with the details shown on the screen, it becomes much easier to use the program facilities and to troubleshoot problems.

Remember to check the Windows Taskbar as well. This shows you how many documents you have open.

Optimise your view

You can easily change the view from Normal to Print layout, so use the view that you are most comfortable with.

Word provides you with several ways to see your document as you work. You can select the style of window and manage features that are available to suit your own preferences.

1. Normal view lets you see the maximum typing area. Print Layout view shows you the text as it will appear on the paper, including margin area. To change views select View from the menu bar.

It is a good idea to adjust your view of the typing page so that you can see as much text at once as possible.

2. You can also change views by selecting the view you want from the Views bar at the bottom of the screen.

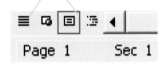

Page 1   Sec 1

Standard and Formatting toolbars are accessed through the View, Toolbars option.

3. Also using the View menu, you can select to show the ruler at the top of the typing area. The ruler shows the typing width that you are using. Initially, this may not seem important, but at some point in the exercise you may be asked to change the width of the margins. From the ruler you can see the associated change in the typing width.

The ruler always starts at zero, whichever view you use. The margins themselves are not included in the measurement.

4. On the previous page we saw the Word window with the Task Pane showing. You can choose to have the task pane open or closed by selecting it from the View menu. The presence of a tick indicates that the task pane is active. Clicking the entry again removes the tick (and removes the Task Pane from the list of toolbars).

Even if you have a version of Word that does not have a Task Pane, the functions are still available through the menus and toolbars.

5 The relevant Task Pane appears automatically when you perform certain activities, such as cut and paste or inserting Clip Art. Each task pane presents you with a group of activities, and the option to view other panes.

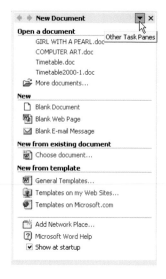

6 The Word window on page 26 also shows the Standard and Formatting toolbars, each on a separate row. To make them share the same row, and free up more viewable typing area, select View, Toolbars, Customise, and then the Options tab.

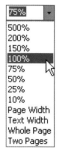

7 You will also see on this menu that you can select large icons.

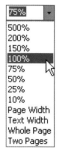

If you wish, you can choose to show shortcut keys in the ScreenTips. This is a good way to become familiar with the keyboard shortcuts.

8 The Show ScreenTips option, selected here, tells you the purpose of the buttons on the toolbars when you hover the mouse over them, a useful feature if you find the buttons difficult to interpret.

9 One other item that may help with your view of the Word window, is the zoom level. You can select an entry from the drop down list, or you can experiment with typing a percentage into the box.

Page layout

Once you have opened Word, and have your window ready for typing, you may want to set the page margins. You will find that the left and right margins are already set at a default value of either 2.54 or 3.17 cms (1 or 1.5 inches).

Margins are set for a whole page. If you want to indent just a single paragraph, then use Format, Paragraph, Indents and Spacing or use the Increase Indent button. See page 47.

The most recently-used tab in a dialog box, is the one that will be foremost when you reopen the dialog box.

1 Select File, Page Setup.

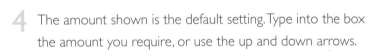

2 Make sure the Margins tab on the Page Setup dialog box is selected.

3 You are usually required to change the left and right margins. The top and bottom margins are seldom changed.

4 The amount shown is the default setting. Type into the box the amount you require, or use the up and down arrows.

5 Note that the Page Setup dialog box also allows you to change the orientation of your paper from portrait to landscape.

6 Click the OK button. When you return to the document, you will find the typing width shown on the horizontal ruler has changed.

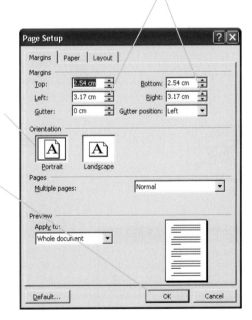

Enter text

Now you are ready to type. As you type, the cursor, a vertical bar indicating the printing point, will travel across the screen. Continue typing even when you reach the right-side edge and the text will wrap onto the next line. When you reach the end of the paragraph, press Enter. Press Enter again for another blank line, and continue with the next paragraph.

There are certain accepted standards in typing, and the New CLAiT 2006 course adheres to them.

- one blank space between words
- one blank space after a comma
- one or two spaces after a full stop, question mark or exclamation mark
- paragraphs must start at the left margin, and not be indented unless specified, even by a single blank
- one clear blank line between paragraphs
- one or two clear blank lines under a heading

Creating blank lines

To create a blank line, use the Enter key. To create a break in the middle of a paragraph, put the cursor just before the first letter of the new paragraph, and press Enter twice. The first Enter splits the paragraph, the second Enter gives the clear blank line between the paragraphs.

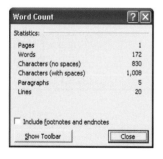

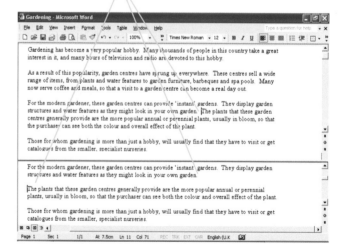

Editing text

Insert and overtype

Word has two typing modes, insert and overtype. Normally when you open Word it is set to insert mode, which means that if you wish to insert another word in the middle of some text, you just position the cursor where you want the word, and type. The text to the right will be pushed along, and where necessary will automatically wrap onto the next line.

If you press the Insert key on the keyboard, it switches to Overtype mode, and any words that you type will replace the existing text.

Delete text

For individual letters or small amounts of text, you can use the backspace or delete keys as appropriate – it just depends where the cursor is in relation to the text you wish to edit.

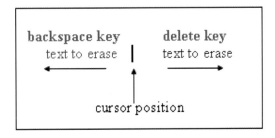

When you wish to delete sentences or larger amounts of text, select the text first and press the delete key. For more information on selecting text see page 38.

The backspace and delete key will remove blank lines, or part blank lines. If the cursor is at the left margin or at the end of a paragraph, press delete and the following blank line or lines will be removed. If the cursor is at the beginning of the next paragraph, press backspace, and blank lines above the cursor will be removed.

Show/hide

The Show/hide button reveals spaces, tabs and paragraph symbols (Enter key), see page 32. Use this feature to ensure that you have the correct spacing between words, and that you have only pressed Enter at the right margin when you need to start a new paragraph.

The Show/hide facility is especially useful when editing fully justified text, as it is difficult to check the spacing between words.

Tab   Paragraph symbol   Spaces

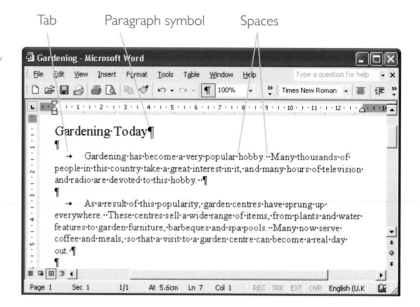

The Undo facility

As you work, Word keeps a running log of your actions. This means that if you wish, you can actually reverse or undo the action. Once you have Undone an action, you can then also Redo the action. Word continues to log your actions until you close the file.

You cannot undo saving a file. If you wish to keep the original version, you must use Save As and give the file a different name.

1 You can select Edit, Undo from the menu, or click on the Undo button.

2 If you wish to undo a series of actions, then click on the down arrow next to the Undo symbol. You can only undo actions in the same sequence in which they were executed.

3 When you close the document, the record of actions is discarded and you start afresh.

The Spell Checker

Press the F7 Function key to invoke the Spell Checker.

The spell check program is normally enabled when you start Word. You will find that any misspelled words are underlined in red, and grammatical or spacing errors are underlined in green. When you are ready to make the corrections:

1 Select Tools, Spelling or Grammar, or click on the button.

Make sure that the Spell check dictionary is set to UK English. You may find that it is set to ignore words in capitals or words with numbers, so you should check these carefully.

2 The misspelled word will be shown in red, with the suggestion(s) for the correction in the lower pane.

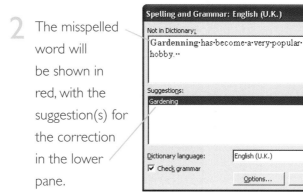

The Grammar check will make suggestions for alternative wording. It is important that you copy the text as shown in the exercise and ignore any grammar changes. However it is useful to identify extra spaces between words and punctuation errors.

3 Select the Change button, if you wish, and the spell checker will automatically move to the next misspelled word

4 You can add the word to the dictionary (Add to Dictionary button), a good idea if it is frequently used, such as the name of your town, or a technical term.

5 Word will tell you when the check is complete.

6 If you wish you can spell check words individually as you type. Click with the right mouse button on the word, and you will be given the spelling suggestions immediately.

There is no substitute for proof reading. The Spell Checker will not find words that are spelled correctly but out of context, such as 'from' instead of 'form', or 'the' instead of 'they'.

Save your document

When you have typed in your text, and even at some point before you have finished, you should save your document. You may find that Word does an autosave at set intervals, but you still need to formally save your document with a name.

1   Press Ctrl+S, or select File, Save or click on the diskette button.

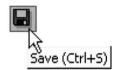

Save (Ctrl+S)

2   The Save As dialog box appears as the file has not yet been saved and has no name or defined location.

3   Check the Save in folder name. If you wish to save it to a different drive or folder, select it now.

For more detail on navigating folders, see page 20.

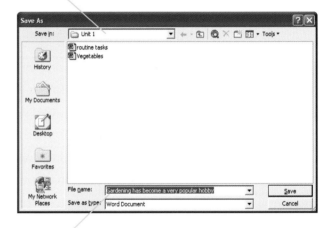

4   The first line of the document has been used as the file name. You could accept the name and just click on Save. However, as the name is so long, it would be sensible to abbreviate or amend it.

5   To change the name, just type – the text highlighted in blue will disappear. If you wish to abbreviate it, click in the bar and use the normal editing keys. Then press Save.

Save with the same file name

It's a good idea to save the file frequently. Once the file has a name and folder or drive location you can simply press Ctrl+S, or click on the diskette symbol as shown on the previous page. This will overwrite the original file with the additional or amended data.

Save with new file name

As part of the New CLAiT 2006 word processing unit, when you have amended your document you are required to save it with a different name. To do this you must use the Save As function.

Press the F12 Function key to take you straight into the Save As command.

1   Select File, Save As. There is no toolbar button for this function.

2   The Save As dialog box that opens is as shown on the previous page.

3   Amend the name as required. Remember, if the file name is highlighted in blue, it will disappear when you begin to type. If you click in the file name box, the highlight disappears but leaves the existing name for you to amend.

You can use the Save As command to save a copy of the file to a different drive or folder location.

4   Make sure you save the file with the name exactly as specified in the exercise, with no extra blanks or characters, as this is also marked.

Save as new file type

You can use the Save or Save As commands to save the file as a different type, if for example you wished to create a plain text file (.txt) for use in another program or with a text editor. However, this is not part of the New CLAiT 2006 syllabus and should be avoided, since the file will lose formatting.

Close the file and program

 The Taskbar shows which applications you have open. Click on the application name and it will list the files you have open.

To close an individual file, but leave the application open:

Close Window

1 Click on the lower Close Window button on the right of the window, or select File, Close.

2 If you have not already saved the file, or if you have made any changes since the last save, you will be prompted to save now.

 You can right click a file on the Taskbar and select Close from that menu. If the file has been modified it will ask if you wish to save.

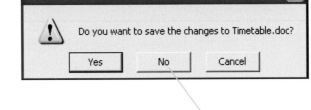

3 To keep the changes, click Yes, to discard the changes click No. Any alterations made to the file since the last Save will be lost.

 If you are working on a floppy disk, then you must close those files before you remove the disk. Otherwise, the application will prompt you to re-insert the disk before it will close.

4 When you have Word open but no document files open, the main typing area will be shown in grey, and most of the buttons will not function. Click on the New button to start a new document.

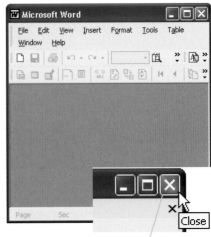
Close

 If you select File, New you are presented with options for different Word templates by the New Document task pane. If you click on the New blank document button, you get the standard document format.

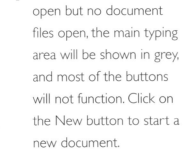

5 To close the application completely, select File, Exit, or click on the Close button at the top right of the screen.

Open an existing file

You can use the Open file function in all Microsoft Office applications to open existing files. Within this function you can navigate between drives and folders to select the required file.

All applications apply filters to the Open and Save windows. This means that you will usually see the normal file type for that application. If the file you want is not visible, check that you have opened the correct application.

I In the application, select File, Open, or click on the Open folder button. The Open window lists files in the current folder. Because Word is our example application, it shows .doc files and any subfolders.

2 Select the file that you want and click the Open button. Alternatively you can double click on the file.

3 If the file is in a subfolder, click on the subfolder and then the Open button, or again double click.

Click on the down arrow on the Files of type box and select All files to see a complete list of files in the folder.

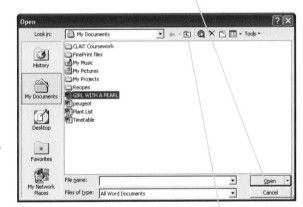

You can use the navigation buttons in the left panel to go straight to the folders listed.

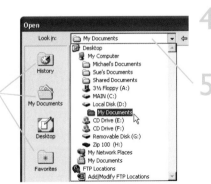

4 Press the Up One Level button to go to a parent folder.

5 Click in the Look in box to navigate to other possible locations, including other drives or files held on a network. In the 'Look in' box, you only need to single click to open the required drive or folder.

Select text

Before looking at text formatting (see page 39), you should first become familiar with selecting portions of text. When text is selected it is shown in reverse video, or highlighted, ready for you to perform actions to change its appearance etc. There are several ways to select text:

If you press Enter when text is highlighted or selected, it will be deleted. If this happens, click the Undo button.

Double click a word to select just the word.

Ctrl+A selects everything in the document.

1 To select a whole line, such as a title, position the mouse arrow in the left margin, so it is pointing at the text, then click with the left mouse button.

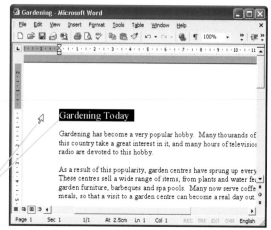

2 To select several lines or a whole paragraph, position the cursor in the left margin, at the beginning of the text. Click and drag down, or up, staying in the left margin.

Avoid dragging across the text with the mouse to highlight it. If the mouse arrow changes direction, you could move the text inadvertently. If this does happen, just click on the Undo button.

3 To select text in the middle of a paragraph, click at the beginning of the text, hold down the Shift key and click at the end of the required text.

4 For individual words, or if you find controlling the mouse difficult, you can use the keyboard. Position the cursor at the beginning of the required text and hold down the Shift key while you press the arrow keys. You can also use the Home and End keys

Use Shift and the arrow keys to select text that extends beyond the top or bottom boundaries of the screen. It gives you much more control and you can continue to select text one line at a time, that would otherwise be out of sight.

5 To remove the highlight, just click anywhere that is not highlighted..

Format text

See page 27 for instructions on how to view the Formatting toolbar.

Formatting text means changing the way it appears on the page. It may for example be underlined, italicised or made larger. You can apply formatting to the text once you have finished typing, or you can initiate a format change so that the new formatting appears as you type.

To apply colour, select the text and click on the button. To select a different colour, click on the down arrow.

1. To change the font style and size, select the text you wish to alter. The current font style is Times New Roman. Click the down arrow to view alternatives, and click on your choice. See page 136 for more information on font types.

In the CLAiT exercise, when you are asked to change the font on a specified section of text, make sure that the font is obviously different.

Font style   Font type   Font size

2. Bold, Italic and Underline are toggle switches. Select the text and click on one or a combination of the buttons. If you wish to remove an effect, re-select the text and click that format button again.

3. Select Format, Font from the menu bar to view the full range of formats that you can apply. You can select the underline style, subscript and superscript. The Preview panel shows the effect of the format change.

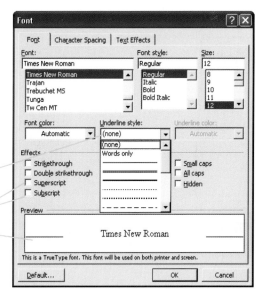

The Format painter allows you to copy a format from one piece of text to another. Position the cursor in the required formatted text. Single click the button to apply formatting once, double click to apply formatting several times. The cursor becomes a brush. Click on text to apply the format. Click the button again when finished.

Alignment and line spacing

Text can be aligned in four ways:

Left aligned –   the text is straight at the left margin and ragged on the right margin. This is how text will be normally aligned when you open Word.

Centred –   when you centre text using the centre function, the text stays centred even when you change the margin width.

Use the Show/ hide button to check the spacing between words when you specify fully justified text (see page 31).

Right aligned – the text is straight at the right margin, ragged at the left. This is mainly used for addresses at the head of letters.

Justified –   the text is straight at both margins. To achieve this Word has to stretch the spaces between the text. Therefore it sometimes appears that you have more than one space between words.

left align (currently selected)   right align   line spacing

Centre

Justified

✓	1.0
	1.5
	2.0
	2.5
	3.0
	More...

1   To change the alignment, just position the cursor in the line or paragraph, and click on the button of choice.

When you select the whole document and change the alignment, you will find that centred titles become left aligned.

2   The alignment buttons are not toggle switches. To reset or change to another layout you must make another selection.

3   You can use Ctrl+A to select the whole document and then use the alignment button.

If this button is not available, select Format, Paragraph. You can specify Line spacing on the Indents and Spacing tab.

4   For line spacing, again, just position the cursor in the paragraph and select from the list. Choosing More takes you to the Format Paragraph dialog box, where you can specify your own.

Move and copy text

To move text from one position to another:

Page 38 describes the various ways provided for selecting the text you wish to move or copy.

1 Select or highlight the text you want to move. Remember to check the spacing at the beginning or end of the text you have selected. You must make sure that the spacing that is left when you remove the text is correct.

2 Click on the Cut button to 'cut' the text from the page, or you can select Edit, Cut from the menu bar. The selected text will disappear and the remaining text will realign.

The keyboard shortcut for Cut is Ctrl+X. The text you remove is placed in the Clipboard area (see page 42).

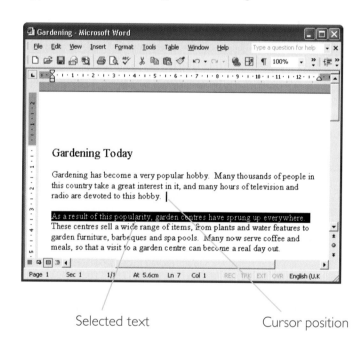

Selected text   Cursor position

When you cut and paste text, check to make sure that your text still wraps correctly at the right margin.

3 Position the cursor where you wish to insert the text. Make sure that the cursor is flashing as a normal vertical bar.

4 Use Edit, Paste or click on the Paste button. The text will be inserted at the cursor point, and the existing text will be realigned to make space. Again, check the spacing to make sure it is correct.

To copy text, use a similar procedure:

Select the text and click on the Copy button.
This time the text stays in place, and it looks like nothing has happened. However, a copy of the selected text has been placed in the Clipboard and the Paste button is now activated.

Keyboard short cuts for copy and paste are: Ctrl+C to copy, Ctrl+V to paste.

Position the cursor where you wish to place a copy of the text, and click on the Paste button.

The Clipboard

To move and copy text, the computer uses the Clipboard facility. This is a utility that holds information in memory until the computer is shut down. The data that you have selected to cut or copy, can be reused in the same application, or it can be transferred to another.

The Clipboard holds up to 24 items, and then the next item copied will replace the oldest item in the Clipboard.

You can manage data in the Clipboard by viewing the Clipboard task pane.

Position the cursor in the document where you wish to paste the text. Then click on the item in the task pane that you require. The text will be inserted immediately.

A Clipboard Smart Tag will appear below the pasted text. Click on the down arrow to view the options. When you continue typing the tag disappears.

Find and replace

As part of the CLAiT exercise, you will be required to replace a particular word, using the Find and Replace function.

The Find and Replace commands are less used, so may not appear when you first click on Edit. Wait for the full Edit menu to appear, or click on the symbol at the bottom of the list.

1 From the menu, select Edit, Replace. This takes you to the same dialog box as the Find command, but the Replace tab will be foremost.

2 In the Find what box, type in the appropriate word. Word will look for all forms of the target word so you do not need to be concerned about capitalisation.

When you click on the More button, it changes to a Less button. This allows you to see more of your document as it is searched.

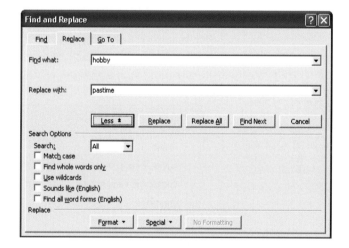

Only select Match case if you wish to limit the search to capitalised words.

3 You can then press the Tab key, or click in the Replace with box and type the replacing word. If you type without capitals, Word will capitalise the replacing word as appropriate.

It is a good idea to avoid Replace All until you see how the Replace function is working, especially in older versions of Word, where capitalisation is treated differently.

4 Click on the Find next button. If you do not wish to replace the word, click again on Find next. If you do wish to replace the word, click on Replace and Word will automatically move to the next occurrence.

Headers and footers

Headers and footers use the top and bottom margin areas on the document. Details added to these areas will appear on every page of the document, with the exception of the first page where you can choose to include or exclude them. They enable you to add useful information that will be updated automatically, such as the page number, current date or the filename. To create a header or footer on your document:

Once you have created a header or footer, you can double click in the header or footer area and skip the Menu.

1 Select View, Header and Footer. The cursor will be visible in the Header area, and the toolbar displayed.

2 You can type into the Header or Footer area to add details such as your name, and you can use Autotext to create entries that will be updated automatically.

When you add an automatic filename using Autotext, the name displayed in the header or footer area will initially state the Word Document number. It will only display the filename when the file has been saved. You should therefore save the file before you print.

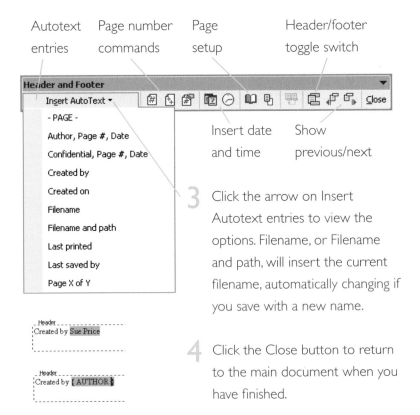

Autotext entries | Page number commands | Page setup | Header/footer toggle switch

Header and Footer

Insert AutoText ▾

- PAGE -
Author, Page #, Date
Confidential, Page #, Date
Created by
Created on
Filename
Filename and path
Last printed
Last saved by
Page X of Y

Close

Insert date and time | Show previous/next

Most Office programs use field codes as placeholders for data that might change in a document. They are used for example, in form letters and mail merge documents. They underpin the Autotext entries that are available in Headers and Footers. Right click on an Autotext entry and select Toggle Field Codes to see the underlying variable.

3 Click the arrow on Insert Autotext entries to view the options. Filename, or Filename and path, will insert the current filename, automatically changing if you save with a new name.

Header
Created by Sue Price

Header
Created by { AUTHOR }

4 Click the Close button to return to the main document when you have finished.

Tables

Create

Tables allow you to manage columns and rows of text easily. You can apply varying alignment or format styles to cells or columns, move individual cell contents, and insert, delete and even split or combine table components.

1 Position the cursor where you want the table. On the Menu bar select Table, Insert, Table.

2 Use the arrows to increase or decrease the number of columns and rows. Click on OK when finished.

Initially the Insert Table button only offers a table size of 5 columns by 4 rows. Continue dragging past the boundary shown and the number of each will be increased.

3 As an alternative, you can use the Insert Table button on the toolbar. Press the left mouse button and drag the mouse pointer across the cells until you have the required numbers. Then release the button.

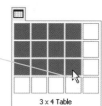

3 x 4 Table

4 You can select the whole table, columns or rows, or individual cells.

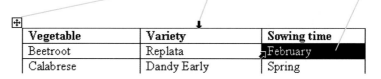

Vegetable	Variety	Sowing time
Beetroot	Replata	February
Calabrese	Dandy Early	Spring

To access the table functions, such as insert columns and rows, the cursor must be within the table.

5 To insert rows and columns, position the cursor in the table next to where you wish to insert. Select Table, Insert, Columns or Rows as appropriate.

6 To add more rows as you fill the table, press the Tab key in the bottom right cell. To move from cell to cell press the Tab key.

Word will adjust the cell depth automatically to accommodate text as you type. To change the cell width, move the mouse to the column markers on the Ruler, click and drag using the double headed arrow.

Move Table Column

Table grid lines will always show when you are working in either Normal or Print layout view. They may, however, not actually print, it depends on how Word has been set up. To check if they will print, select Print Preview.

Grid lines

To enable borders and lines:

1   Position the cursor inside the table and select Table, Table Properties.

Use the other tabs on this menu to view the options for page borders, shading effects.

2   With the Table tab selected, click on the Borders and Shading button. Now choose from the preset options on the left, such as None or All, or select individually and preview the effect on the right.

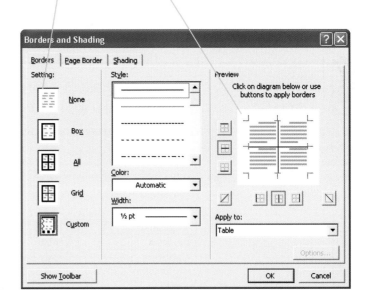

The Borders button icon will change to reflect the most recently chosen option.

3   The Borders button provides a useful shortcut. You can choose one or more of the options. In the example shown, internal grid lines only are selected.

4   Use Print Preview to check the effect.

Vegetable	Variety	Sowing time
Beetroot	Replata	February
Calabrese	Dandy Early	Spring
Carrot	Nantes Express	March
Dwarf French Beans	Aramis	April

Tabs and indents

L   Left tab

⊥   Centre tab

⌐   Right tab

⊥.   Decimal tab

Tabs are a quick and easy way to line up text in columns or to indent the first line in a paragraph. Default tab stops are set at every 1.27 cms, as shown on the Ruler. Press the Tab key on the keyboard to move to the setting. To define your own settings:

1. Position the cursor before the text where you want the new tab settings to start. Select Format, Tabs.

2. Type the required tab position into the Tab stop box, and choose the alignment: left, centred etc.

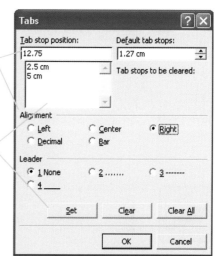

3. Click the Set button and the tab setting will be moved to the lower pane. Repeat the process for each tab position, selecting the alignment for each tab. When finished, click OK.

4. To delete or change a setting, select the Tab stop position in the left pane, and change the alignment, or select Clear.

You can also use the Ruler to set tabs, although it is not as easy to be accurate with the positioning.

5. Cycle through the tab types at the left of the Ruler. When you see the one you want, click on the Ruler in the desired position.

Bullets and numbering

Bullets and numbering work in the same way so the techniques that you learn for one can be applied to the other.

You can apply bullets to the text as you type, but it is generally easier to apply bullets after the text has been created.

1 Select the text to be bulleted or numbered, then click the Bullets or Numbering button on the toolbar.

2 To add more items to the bulleted list, just press Enter at the end of the last item. A new bullet point is automatically created.

3 To revert to normal text, press Enter twice, or move to a new line and click on the selected button to turn the facility off.

Using the Menu to apply bullets or numbering allows you to change the bullet point or the numbering style and the indentation.

On the Bullets and Numbering window, select None to turn Bullets off.

4 Select the text and click Format, Bullets and Numbering. Select a new style from the options or click on the Customise button to change the bullet point style and indentation.

To amend the indentation of Bullets and Numbering quickly, select the bulleted text and click on the Increase or Decrease Indent button on the Tool bar.

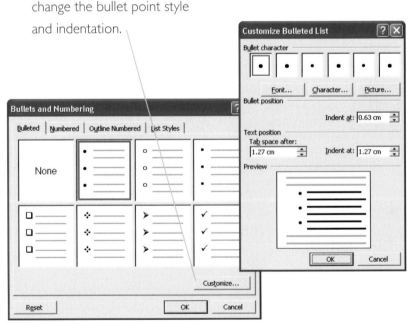

Print preview

When its time to print, use Print Preview. It is a very valuable tool, saving you wasted paper, and also time.

1 Select Print Preview on the toolbar.

2 You will now see your document as it will appear when printed. If the text is very small you can zoom in to read it, although the Print Preview window is used primarily to view the layout.

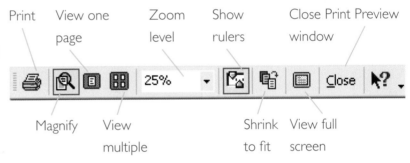

Print View one page

Zoom level

Show rulers

Close Print Preview window

Magnify View multiple

Shrink to fit View full screen

3 Selecting the Print button will bypass the Print dialog box and start the printing process immediately. View Multiple Pages lets you see up to fifteen pages at once, or use the Next and Previous Page buttons to scroll through the document. Click with the mouse anywhere on the text to zoom in and out on the document.

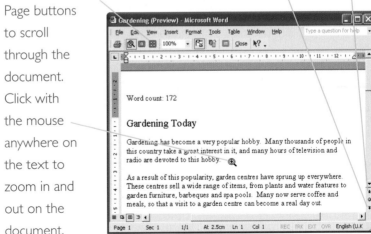

Print your file

Most New CLAiT 2006 exercises only require you to print one page.

You can print your file directly from the Print Preview window, or by clicking on the Printer button, but to control the printing process, and change any of the defaults, such as the printer, you need to use the Print Dialog box.

1 To open the Print dialog box, select File, Print.

You can check to see if your printer is set to use A4 paper by clicking the Properties button.

2 If you have more than one printer attached, select the printer.

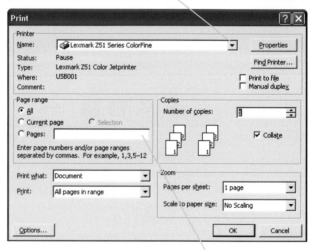

If you want to print one page only, position the cursor somewhere on the page you want and select to print current page.

3 The set option is to print the whole document. You may wish to print only certain pages. Click in the Pages button, and type your selection. For individual pages, type the page numbers separated by commas, e.g. 2,5,8. For consecutive pages separate them with a hyphen, e.g. 2-8.

Printing in colour is discussed in Unit 4 (see page 143) and Unit 6 (see page 183).

4 Other options include specifying number of copies and how many pages per sheet. When you have completed your selection, click OK and the printing will start.

Your printer

To see which printers are attached to your computer, select Start, Control Panel, Printers and Faxes. This opens the Printers folder.

1   In this folder you will see the Printer Tasks frame with printing controls. Add a Printer starts the wizard which guides you through the installation process.

2   You may find more than one printer installed on your computer. You can have both local printers and network printers. The default printer is indicated by a tick symbol on its icon.

3   The Details frame shows the status of the selected printer. For more information, select the printer, right click (click with the right mouse button) and choose Properties.

Open Printer properties, click the Paper tab, and check that the paper size is set to A4 in the UK.

4   When you select print in an application, the printer icon will appear in the Notification Area on the taskbar. This provides you with a shortcut to the printer that is only available whilst the printer is active.

You can use Task bar settings to add the printers folder directly to the Start menu.

Managing the printer

Printing is a three stage process. The document is formatted by the application. The results are passed to a holding area, known as the print spool. Then the information is transferred progressively to the printer. If it is just a brief text document, it will probably print before you are able to cancel. With longer documents or pictures, however, it is possible to pause or cancel the print.

1 Double click the printer icon in the Notification area to open the printer folder. Click the button to expand Printer Tasks.

2 To pause a document, select Pause printing. The option changes to Resume printing.

3 To see which documents are still waiting to be printed, select See what's printing. This opens the printer window and displays the list of files in the print queue.

It's best to avoid turning the printer off whilst it is printing.

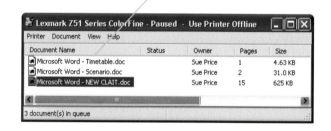

4 To cancel the print, select the file, and from the menu bar select Document, Cancel.

If you are using a network printer, you may find it slow to respond to instructions to pause or cancel.

5 If the printer is switched off, or out of paper you will get a warning message. When you switch on or load paper, the printer may well start to print without further action as it is usually set to retry automatically.

Print folder contents

Windows Explorer does not offer a specific print function to enable you to print the contents of the drives and folders as lists, or show the organisation of nested folders and their content. To achieve a print of your folder structure and contents:

1 Open the Explorer window, and select and open the folder in the left pane so that the contents are shown on the right.

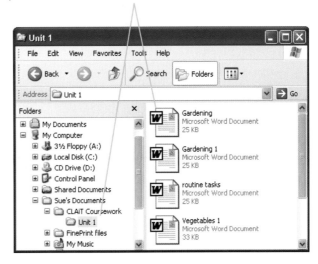

2 Shrink the window to a reasonable size using the Resize button.

3 Using the keyboard, press Alt and Print Screen together. This will place a copy of the active window into the Clipboard.

4 Open Word, and use the Edit, Paste facility. The copied screen will be pasted into the Word document. Repeat the process for each folder, to add a screen copy of each to the Word document.

5 You can then add your name, and other required details, and save and print the Word document.

Shutdown

When you have finished working, it is very important that you close down the computer properly. While you have been working, the operating system has been running in the background, managing memory usage and the storage of files. When you use the correct closing procedure, Windows is able to ensure that all the temporary files it has created are erased and its own system files are closed.

If you turn off the computer without using the correct Shut Down procedure, you will find that the next time you turn on the computer, the ScanDisk program will run to check out the system.

1   Check the Taskbar and ensure that all the applications you have been using are now closed.

2   Click the Start button. As separate Users have been defined one User can Log Off, and allow another User to Log On, without closing down the system.

Occasionally you may find that the system freezes and stops responding to the keyboard or mouse. Press Ctrl+Alt+Del simultaneously on the keyboard. This will bring up the Windows Task Manager, and will indicate which program is not responding. You may then be able to close just that program and continue working.

3   Select Turn Off Computer. From the next window you can choose Stand By mode. This allows you to leave the computer switched on but reduce the power consumption. When you return it remembers exactly where you were and you can carry on using the same applications.

4   Restart means you can close down and restart the computer without actually turning it off.

When the Shut Down process is complete, you will get the message 'It is now safe to turn off the computer'.

5   Select Turn Off. Some computers power off automatically, you will not need to switch them off physically. If this happens, the monitor may go into Stand By mode, so you can turn it off independently.

Unit 1 exercise

Before you begin this exercise, download the files from the In Easy Steps web site (see page 253). The procedure will create an NC2006data folder structure as shown, to contain the source files.

You are allowed two and a half hours to complete this assignment.

To begin, you will need to create a folder structure to help organise files created or amended in carrying out the New CLAiT 2006 'in easy steps' exercises.

Task 1

1. Create a folder within My Documents named CLAiT Coursework.
2. In the CLAiT Coursework folder, create a subfolder named Unit 1. The folder structure should be similar to the one illustrated.

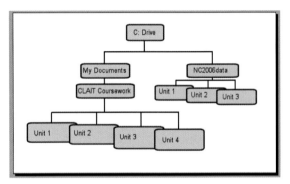

Your manager has asked you create a report for the local gardening club.

Task 2

1. Create a new word processing document.
2. Set the left and right page margins to 3 cms.
3. Enter the following text with a justified left margin and an unjustified right margin.

Gardening Today

Gardening has become a very popular hobby. Many thousands of people in this country take a great interest in it, and many hours of television and radio are devoted to this hobby.

Files are saved by default into My Documents, so it's easier to create the CLAiT Coursework folder there. You can then access exercises in progress by using My Documents from the Start menu, or from the Desktop shortcut.

As a result of this popularity, garden centres have sprung up everywhere. These centres sell a wide range of items, from plants and water features to garden furniture, barbecues and spa pools. Many now serve coffee and meals, so that a visit to a garden centre can become a real day out.

For the modern gardener, these garden centres can provide 'instant' gardens. They display garden structures and water features as they might look in your own garden. The plants that these garden centres generally provide are the more popular annual or perennial plants, usually in bloom, so that the purchaser can see both the colour and overall effect of the plant.

Those for whom gardening is more than just a hobby, will usually find that they have to visit or get catalogues from the smaller, specialist nurseries.

4. Enter your name, an automatic date field and an automatic filename in the footer area.
5. Spell check the document.
6. Perform a word count on the document.
7. Type Word Count: and enter the number into the header area.
8. Format the heading so that it is larger than the rest of the text.
9. Save your report with the filename Gardening into the Unit I subfolder and print one copy.

Task 3

Your manager has asked for the following amendments to be made to the report.

1. Insert a paragraph break and clear linespace in the third paragraph after the words ….in your own garden.
2. Delete the last sentence of the second paragraph.
   Many now serve coffee and meals, so that a visit to a garden centre can become a real day out.
3. Move the first sentence of the second paragraph
   As a result of this popularity, garden centres have sprung up everywhere.
   so that it becomes the last sentence of the first paragraph.

4. Insert the following text as the final sentence of the second paragraph, after the words …barbecues and spa pools.

   Many also carry a wide range of gazebos and conservatories.

Errors mainly arise from not reading the questions properly, missing a step or requirement, or failing to proof-read thoroughly. Always check your final printout as mistakes are much more evident on paper.

5. Replace all occurrences of hobby with pastime (three times in all).

6. Change only the heading Gardening Today to a different font.

7. Embolden and centre the heading Gardening Today. Ensure the rest of the text in not emboldened.

8. Fully justify all the text apart from the heading.

9. Save the report with the new filename Gardening 1 into the Unit 1 subfolder and print one copy of the report.

Task 4

To complete this part of the exercise you will need the following files from the NC2006data folder:
Vegetables.doc
Routine.doc

1. Copy the file Vegetables.doc from the Unit 1 subfolder in the NC2006data folder into the Unit 1 subfolder in the CLAiT coursework folder in My Documents.

2. Open the file and add the following title and table at the end of the bulleted list.

Fast Varieties for Catch and Inter-cropping

Vegetable	Variety	Sowing Time
Beetroot	Replata	February
Calabrese	Dandy Early	Spring
Carrot	Nantes Express	March
Dwarf French Beans	Aramis	April
Lettuce	Little Gem	May
Radish	Ribella	Every three weeks
Spinach	All varieties	Spring
Turnip	Snowball	February

3. Embolden the title and table headings – Vegetable, Variety and Sowing Time.

4. Add a 2¼ pt border around the whole table.

5. Change the bulleted text to numbered items.

6. Add your name, and an automatic file name and page number to the header area.
7. Save the report with the new file name Vegetables 1.
8. Print a final copy of the report and close the document.

Task 5

1. Copy the file name Routine from the Unit 1 subfolder of the NC2006data folder to the subfolder Unit 1 of the CLAiT Coursework folder.
2. Rename the file Routine Tasks.
3. Open the file Routine Tasks and change the page orientation to landscape. Centre the title.
4. Change the font for months April to October to a sans serif font.
5. Change the top and bottom margins to 2 cms.
6. Indent the paragraph beginning 'Winter prune fruit trees'....
7. Set the whole document in 1.5 line spacing.
8. Add your name and an automatic file name in the footer area.
9. Save the file as Routine Tasks into the Unit 1 subfolder.
10. Print the file in landscape orientation.

Task 6

1. Create a screen print of the CLAiT Coursework folder.
2. Create a screen print of the Unit 1 subfolder.
3. Add your name and an automatic date field to the header area.
4. Save the file with the name Screenprint.
5. Print the Screenprint file and close the document.

You should have the following files and printouts:

Gardening	Gardening 1
Vegetables 1	Routine Tasks

Screen prints of the CLAiT Coursework folder and the Unit 1 subfolder.

Creating Spreadsheets and Graphs

This unit covers using the Excel spreadsheet to enter, edit and present numerical data. It includes creating, copying and printing formulae. It also explains the generation and management of graphs.

Unit Two

Covers

The spreadsheet | 60

Change the layout | 63

Creating formulae | 67

Functions | 68

The Fill tool | 72

Copying formulae | 73

Numeric format | 75

Borders and shading | 77

Headers and footers | 78

Printing spreadsheets | 80

Charts | 82

Create pie, bar and line charts | 84

Editing charts | 90

Troubleshooting | 93

Changing segment display | 95

Printing charts | 96

Unit 2 exercise | 97

The spreadsheet

To start Excel, select Start, All Programs, Microsoft Excel.

Excel can also be used as a database program as it has search, sort and query functions.

The spreadsheet design is based on the ledger sheet. Information is entered in columns and rows, with each cell (the intersection of a column and a row) containing one item of data. Each cell has a cell reference or address, A1, B6, etc. The spreadsheet has columns from A-Z, AA-AZ, BA-BZ and so on and 65,000 rows. The spreadsheet window has both familiar features and new ones.

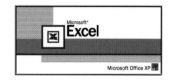

1 The window has the usual Title Bar, Menu bar and Toolbar, with the Standard and Formatting bars sharing one row. We can also see the Task Pane, with its various options.

To put Standard and Formatting bars on separate rows to see more buttons, click on

2 The Formula bar shows the cursor position as a cell reference, in this case A1. It will also show the data contents of the cell.

The current cell (and typing location/cursor) is the black rectangle.

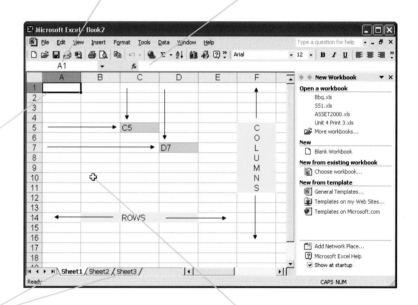

The spreadsheet is known as a Workbook, it normally has three sheets, but you can add more. To move to another sheet, just click on the tab.

3 The mouse takes the shape of a large + which floats over the spreadsheet grid. You must click on a cell to make it the active or current cell, as referenced in the formula bar.

A cell address always begins with a letter, e.g. C5.

Work in the spreadsheet is based on the cell. You enter data into cells and use their cell address as a reference. Later in the unit, you will learn how to use the cell address in formulae.

A series of consecutive cells is known as a range. A range can consist of part of a row or column or a combination of both.

4 The range identified in green is B4:D4. The colon in the range reference means include all the cells in between.

To select a range, press the left mouse button and drag to cover the required cells.

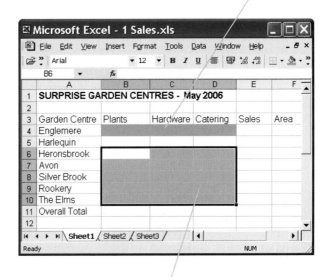

Cell references can be typed in upper or lower case.

You can name a range of cells and use it as a reference point to go to in the spreadsheet, or use it in formula. This is not a New CLAiT 2006 Level 1 requirement.

5 The range coloured blue is B6:D10. This range has been selected with the mouse. The white cell, B6, is the starting point of the selection. The first cell in any selection will always remain white.

6 When you are working with a large spreadsheet, larger than screen-size, you will lose sight of your row or column labels as you scroll down or to the right. To fix them so they remain visible, position the cursor below and to the right of the labels, B4 in the sample shown above, and select Window, Freeze Panes.

To Unfreeze panes, just select Window, Unfreeze Panes from any location on the sheet.

Create a spreadsheet

Excel files have the three letter extension .xls.

When you have typed in a cell, you can press an arrow key. This inserts the data and moves the cursor to the next cell in that direction.

For the New CLAiT 2006 course you will only need to create a small spreadsheet, with straightforward formulae. To enter data:

1. Type the spreadsheet title in cell A1. You must press Enter for it to be inserted. The cursor moves automatically down one cell. For this reason, you may find it easier to enter the data in columns.

2. You should normally enter the data into consecutive cells, without leaving any empty columns or rows, although a blank row under the title is acceptable.

The Formula bar shows the full cell contents.

These are the column and row headings (A,B,C, and 1,2,3). The text in column A and above the numbers are referred to as column and row labels.

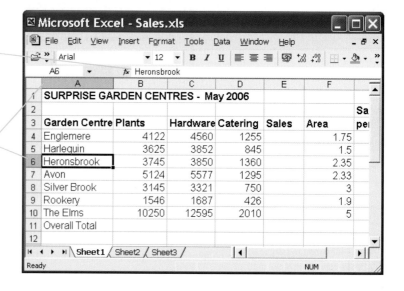

	A	B	C	D	E	F	
1	SURPRISE GARDEN CENTRES - May 2006						
2							Sa
3	Garden Centre	Plants	Hardware	Catering	Sales	Area	pe
4	Englemere	4122	4560	1255		1.75	
5	Harlequin	3625	3852	845		1.5	
6	Heronsbrook	3745	3850	1360		2.35	
7	Avon	5124	5577	1295		2.33	
8	Silver Brook	3145	3321	750		3	
9	Rookery	1546	1687	426		1.9	
10	The Elms	10250	12595	2010		5	
11	Overall Total						
12							

3. As you enter data into the cells, you will see that text is always left aligned, and numbers right aligned. Decimals are displayed as typed.

Data input of numbers in the spreadsheet must be 100% correct.

4. To amend an entry, you can just retype it. You can also double click a cell or press F2, both of which will position the cursor within the cell for you to make changes, or even edit in the Formula bar.

Change the layout

You will need to make changes to the spreadsheet layout.

When you widen a column, it is widened all the way down the spreadsheet.

1 The columns are not wide enough to display the full cell contents. Where the adjoining cell to the right remains empty, the full text is displayed. Where there is data in the adjoining cell, the full contents remain, but the display is truncated.

2 To widen the column, first click on the widest entry, then select Format, Column, AutoFit Selection.

Make sure that the column is wide enough even when printed. If you add or amend an entry, don't forget to check the column width again.

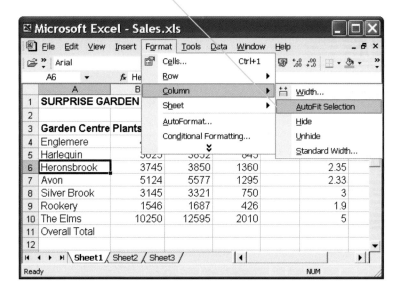

If your column is not wide enough to display all the numeric data, you will see a series of hash signs. Just widen the column to view the data.

3 You can also widen the column by positioning the mouse over the divider on the column heading. When you get the double-headed arrow, double click, or press the left mouse button and drag to the width you require. Notice, however, that the title is the widest entry in column A and double clicking would widen the column to accommodate it, not the row label entries.

Another required change to the layout is to insert or delete columns and rows.

If you insert the new row or column in the wrong place, just click Undo.

1 Columns are inserted to the left of the cursor, and rows above. When you have positioned the cursor, select Insert, and pick columns or rows as appropriate.

If you highlight or select more than one column or row, the number you have chosen will be inserted. See the Hot Tip on page 61 for selecting cells.

2 The inserted column or row will have a Smart Tag attached to it. This facility allows you to apply a format to the column. Click on the Smart Tag to display the Format menu.

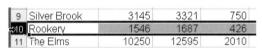

Alignment of the column titles is important in New CLAiT. See page 76 for more information.

3 If you copy the format (from the left or the right column) when you insert a column, your column titles should maintain the alignment you have already chosen.

9	Silver Brook	3145	3321	750
10	Rookery	1546	1687	426
11	The Elms	10250	12595	2010

4 To erase the contents of an entire column or row, first click on the column or row heading. This selects the whole column or row. You can then press the Delete key. The data will be erased, but the column or row remains.

Excel offers the facility to hide columns and rows. However, this only hides the data, the values will still be included in any formulae. When you are instructed to delete a column or row, you must remove it completely.

5 To delete the column or row completely, so that no blank cells remain in the data, select the column or row, as above, and click on Edit and Delete. The row or column disappears, and the adjacent ones slide along to fill the gap.

Once you have typed data into the spreadsheet, you should seldom need to retype it. As well as inserting and deleting columns and rows, you can move the contents of cells.

When you delete a column or row, it affects the whole of the spreadsheet.
Make sure that you do not delete any data that is required but not currently visible.

1 If you select Edit, Delete without selecting a whole column or row, you will be offered the option to move cells. Use this option if you have misaligned your data or want to delete a section of a row, not across the whole width of the spreadsheet.

2 You can move the contents of cells quickly and easily with the mouse pointer. Select a cell or range of cells and position the mouse on any edge of the range. A four-headed arrow appears, and you can then drag and drop to the required position. Any existing data will be over-written.

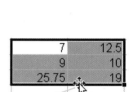

When you insert or delete columns or rows, or if you move cells, Excel automatically adjusts any formulae that reference the range involved. See page 74 for more details on recalculating formulae.

You can also use Cut and Paste to move cells:

3 Select the cells you wish to move. Stay on the selected cells and click with the right mouse button. From the menu, select the entry Cut. The selected cells will be outlined by a flashing box and will remain on the screen.

4 Click on the target cell and select the Paste entry. Pasted cells retain their relative positions.

File management is the same throughout Microsoft Office, so the methods used to Open, Close, Save, and Save As are the same for Excel as Word. See pages 34-37.

5 To remove the flashing outline, press Escape on the keyboard.

Sort

You are not required to sort data for the New CLAiT syllabus. However, it is useful to know how to manipulate and re-organise any data.

Excel has an extensive database facility. It allows you to sort data, by one or several keys. It can apply filters, search for data and let you create complex queries.

When using the database facilities in Excel, you can specify the data range to use. However, it is often worth separating data ranges with blank lines as Excel recognises and works within a data range if it is separate. To use the Sort facility:

1. If you have a separate data area, just position the cursor within the data range. Otherwise, select the required data area. From the Menu choose Data, Sort.

2. When the Sort window opens you should see the selected data range highlighted in the background. Check that it is correct.

3. The Sort window allows you to sort by three levels, and at each level in ascending or descending order. Excel will usually recognise if the columns have a header row, and if so offer the headings in the Sort by box.

4. Select the Options button for further sorting options, if for example you wanted to sort left to right, rather than the more normal top to bottom. Click OK when finished, and check the result on the spreadsheet.

The Undo button will undo an incorrect Sort, which could be very useful if, for example, headings were sorted too in error.

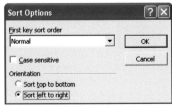

Creating formulae

The spreadsheet formulae work with standard mathematical notation and with cell references. All formulae start with = (an equals sign), this is the indicator to the application that this cell contains a formula.

Remember to position the cursor in the cell where you want the formula (result).

If you are unfamiliar with using brackets in arithmetic, consider the following:

2+2*4=10 (multiply first)

(2+2)*4=16 (brackets first)

Once you have typed an = sign, Excel will let you move the mouse or cursor to select any cell. When you click on a cell you will see the cell reference appear in the formula box.

When you are constructing a formula, only click on cells that you wish to include.
Check your cell references and formulae before you press Enter.

1 A simple formula is: =B4+C4 or as illustrated =E5/F5 When you press

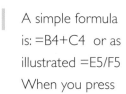

G5	▼		f_x =E5/F5		
	C	D	E	F	G
1	**TRES - May 2006**				
2					Sales
3	Hardware	Catering	Sales	Area	per Hectare
4					
5	4560	1255	9937	1.75	5678.29
6	3852	845	8322	1.5	

Enter, Excel calculates the answer and shows it in the active cell. The Formula bar displays the actual formula. If you change the contents of the referenced cells, the result is recalculated.

2 You can use any operators, + (plus) - (minus) * (multiply) / (divide), and you can use them in combination. The normal rules of mathematical precedence apply, i.e. brackets are calculated first, then multiplication and division, and finally addition and subtraction.

3 It is possible to type the cell references in the formula, but often easier and more accurate to select them with the mouse. First position the cursor in the correct cell, in the example G5. Type an = sign. Click with the mouse on the first cell, E5, type the / (divide) sign, and click with the mouse on the second cell, F5. Press Enter, or click on the tick.

4 If you prefer to use the keyboard, in G5 type = and move the cursor using the arrow keys to E5, type the / and move to F5. Then press Enter.

File	Edit	View	Insert	Format	Tools	Data	Window	Help
»	Arial			▼ 10 ▼	B	I	U	≡ ≡ ≡	🍕
SUM		▼ ✗ ✓ f_x =E5/F5						

	C	D	E	F	G
1	**TRES - May 2006**				
2					Sales
3	Hardware	Catering	Sales	Area	per Hectare
4					
5	4560	1255	9937	1.75	=E5/F5
6	3852	845	8322	1.5	
7	3850	1360	8955	2.35	

Functions

A function carries out a mathematical or statistical calculation.

The example formula shown on the previous page is very simple and straightforward. Most of the formulae you will be required to create in the New CLAiT course will be just as easy, multiplying one cell by another, or dividing one by another, etc.

Excel allows you to use pre-defined functions in the spreadsheet, and it lets you work with ranges of cells in calculations, rather than identifying cell addresses individually. To help you select and use the function you need, Excel provides a Function Wizard.

To view the list of Functions, select the Insert Function button on the Formula bar.

1 The list is divided into categories to make it easier to find an appropriate formula.

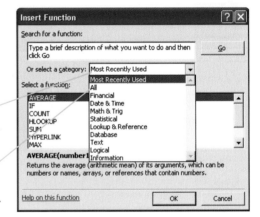

2 Currently showing are the Most Recently Used. To see all possible functions, select All from the list.

3 If you are not sure of which function is appropriate, you can type a description of your requirement and click the Go button.

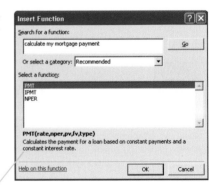

4 The Wizard suggests some possibilities and as you select each one, provides a brief description of how it works.

If you start the AutoSum function and realize your cursor is in the wrong cell, press Esc on the keyboard. Any previous cell contents will be restored.

The AutoSum function is the most commonly used. It adds together columns or rows of figures. You can type it yourself, as with any formula, or you can use the AutoSum function on the toolbar. The Sum function syntax is =SUM(cell reference:cell reference). The (cell reference:cell reference) represents a range of cells, for example E4 to E10. To use AutoSum:

1 Position the cursor in the cell where you wish to place the total or answer. Click the AutoSum button.

Using the Sum function you can add whole columns or rows of figures quickly and easily.

Microsoft Excel - Sales.xls

File Edit View Insert Format Tools Data Window Help

SUM =SUM(E4:E10)

	A	B	C	D	E	F
1	SURPRISE GARDEN CENTRES - May 2006					
2						Sale
3	Garden Centre	Plants	Hardware	Catering	Sales	Area per
4	Englemere	4122	4560	1255	9937	1.75	567
5	Harlequin	3625	3852	845	8322	1.5
6	Heronsbrook	3745	3850	1360	8955	2.35	381
7	Avon	5124	5577	1295	11996	2.33	514
8	Silver Brook	3145	3321	750	7216	3	240
9	Rookery	1546	1687	426	3659	1.9	192
10	The Elms	10250	12595	2010	24855	5
11	Overall Total				=SUM(E4:E10)
12					SUM(number1, [number2], ...)

Sheet1 Sheet2 Sheet3

Point   NUM

2 The AutoSum function will create the formula to total the column of figures above the cursor. You will see the suggested range outlined. Check that it has selected the correct range of cells, and press Enter, or click the tick.

3 The AutoSum function will not include a cell containing text, or an empty cell. It only selects the range up to that point. However, you can re-select the range of cells with the mouse. While the range of cells in the formula is still highlighted (yellow on black), click on the first cell and drag to select the correct range. You will see the cell reference in the brackets change. When it is correct, press Enter.

You must check which cell range AutoSum has selected. It doesn't always get it right.

4 The AutoSum function adds the contents in a row in a similar way. Position the cursor at the end of the row of figures and click the AutoSum button. The figures to the left will be totalled. This only works this way for the first two rows in a column of values.

3	Garden Centre	Plants	Hardware	Catering	Sales	Area	per
4	Englemere	4122	4560	1255	9937	1.75	
5	Harlequin	3625	3852	845	=SUM(B5:D5)		
6	Heronsbrook	3745	3850	1360	SUM(**number1**, [number2],		

You will only use AutoSum for the first row in the spreadsheet. For the rest of the rows you MUST use the Fill by Example feature. See page 73 on copying formulae.

5 When there are no figures, or only one figure, above the cursor, AutoSum will automatically add the row.

3	Garden Centre	Plants	Hardware	Catering	Sales	Area	per
4	Englemere	4122	4560	1255	9937	1.75	
5	Harlequin	3625	3852	845	8322	1.5	
6	Heronsbrook	3745	3850	1360	=SUM(E4:E5)		
7	Avon	5124	5577	1295	SUM(**number1**, [number2], ...)		

6 If there are two or more figures above the cursor, AutoSum will automatically add column-wise.

The Average function is similar in format to the Sum function: =Average(cell address:cell address). To use the Average function:

1 Click on the down arrow next to the AutoSum and select Average.

You don't want the value of Sales (the sum of Plants, Hardware and Catering) included in the Average calculation.

2 Check the range it has selected. In this example, the default selection would give an incorrect result, so you must adjust it.

3	Garden Centre	Plants	Hardware	Catering	Sales	Average	
4	Englemere	4122	4560	1255	9937	=AVERAGE(B4:E4)	
5	Harlequin	3625	3852	845	AVERAGE(**number1**, [number2], ...)		

Many of the functions are complex and require the user to have a mathematical background. Some, like Max, Min and Average are much easier to use and it is a good idea to use one of these to familiarise yourself with how the Insert Function works.

The Function Arguments dialog box attempts to explain the formula. Sometimes its use of jargon is self-defeating.

1 Position the cursor where you want your Average formula. Select Insert Function, choose Average and click OK.

2 The Function Arguments dialog box appears. The black box is the range of cells that it is using in its formula. It shows the actual data selected and the

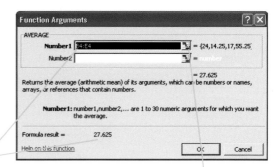

The Arguments are simply the range of cells you wish to use in the formula. You can select a second range of cells to include in the formula if required.

result of the formula. It is always wise to confirm the range it has chosen, so click the Collapse Dialog button.

You must check which cell range the function has selected. It doesn't always get it right.

3 The Function Arguments window remains, but only the selection box is available. As in the previous Average formula, the Total cell is incorrectly included, so use the mouse to re-select the range.

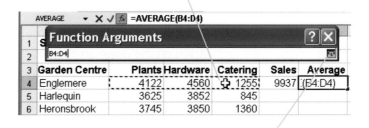

The Collapse dialog feature is used in other Excel areas such as creating charts.

4 Click again on the button to expand the dialog box and return to the Function Argument window. When finished click on OK and you will return to the spreadsheet.

The Fill tool

Excel provides the Fill tool to enable swift data entry of standard items such as days and months, dates, numbers and series of any type. It even allows you to create your own lists, for use with the Fill tool.

1 The Fill option is found in the Edit menu, but is more easily accessed by positioning the mouse on the bottom right corner of the active cell. You will see the mouse symbol change to a black +.

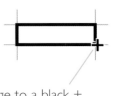

2 To fill a range of cells, select the starting cell and position the mouse on the Fill handle. Press the left mouse button and drag in the direction you wish to fill.

When you fill with months you can start with any month. When you fill with days you can start with any day, and the Fill options offer to fill with just weekdays.

3 As you drag you will get an indication of the fill data. Release the mouse to complete the fill.

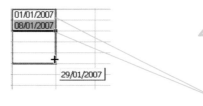

4 You can fill a range with an incremental series. First create and select the pattern, in these examples you will need to select two cells. Use the Fill handle at the bottom of the selection and drag and release as before.

The first option to Copy Cells would have filled the range with just the number one.

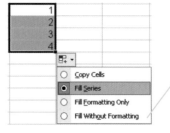

5 When you have filled the range, you will see a smart tag with a range of fill options.

Copying formulae

The spreadsheet works with cell references, which could be a single cell, or a range of cells. In formulae these references are described as relative or absolute.

A relative reference is based on the relative position of cells. So a formula that totals a column is adding the cells above it. A formula that totals a row to the left, is adding the cells to the left of it. The relative reference is the norm.

You are not required to use absolute cell references in New CLAiT.

An absolute reference refers always to a specific cell. To make a reference absolute you must include $ (the dollar sign) as part of the cell reference, for example F7.

When you copy relative formulae the cell references automatically adjust. When you copy formulae that contain absolute references, those cell references remain the same.

To copy formula:

> Select your first formula, whether in the first column or row.

You are required to replicate or copy formulae in CLAiT. The easiest way to do this is with the Fill facility. You could also use copy and paste.

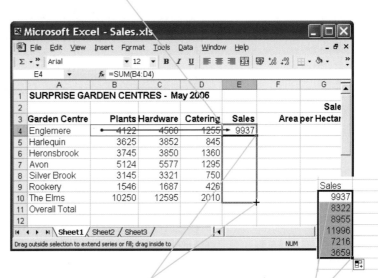

> 2 Use the Fill handle to drag down or across the range of cells, and release. A formula based on the relative position will be copied to each cell and the result calculated.

When you change numeric data in the spreadsheet, formulae that reference those cells will recalculate the result. This also happens when you delete columns and rows.

Recalculate

If you insert a column or row, the insertion point will affect whether or not its data is included. In the example illustrated on the previous page, the formula in E4 references the range B4:D4.

1   If you insert a new column between B and D, the data will be included automatically in the calculation.

2   If you insert a new column between D and E, outside the current range but before the formula, the data will still automatically be included in the calculation. Excel indicates this by moving the cursor to the formula cell.

This is a new feature in Excel 2002 (the Office XP version).

3   If you insert a new column between A and B, this cell is not referenced in the formula and there is no recalculation. However, a small indicator appears top left in the formula cell.

Always check your formulae to make sure they are correct.

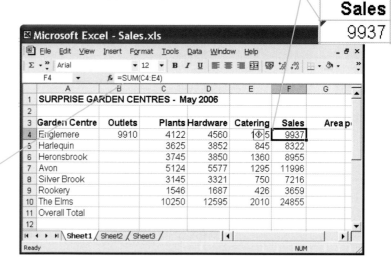

Notice how Excel has adjusted the formula already to recognise the insertion of a column: B4:D4 has become C4:E4.

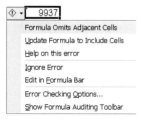

4   When you click on the formula cell, a warning exclamation appears, indicating that the data in the new column has not been included.

Numeric format

At some point during the CLAiT exercise, you will be required to present numbers to a required number of decimal places, and/or with a currency symbol.

To format numbers:

Integer simply means whole numbers with no decimal places.

1 Select the range of cells to format. Remember that the first cell in any selection remains white.

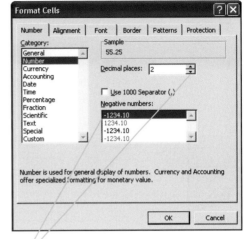

Although numbers may be displayed in integer format, calculations will still be performed using the exact number, including decimal values.

2 Select Format Cells from the menu, and from the Category list click on Number. You can now choose the number of decimal places, to use commas in thousands, and how to display negative numbers.

When you format the column to currency you will need to widen it or you may only see hash signs. See page 63.

3 Select Currency or Accounting to display the £ sign in each cell. The Accounting format aligns the £ symbol to the left of the cell. You can also select the Euro symbol if you wish.

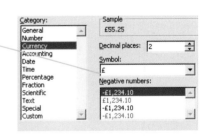

The Currency button on the toolbar is not a toggle switch. If you decide not to use currency format, re-select the cells and choose Format, Cells, General or Number.

4 The Formatting toolbar provides easy access to some formats.

Percentage   Comma   Increase

Currency

Decrease decimal

When using the Increase and Decrease Decimal buttons, you will need to increase decimals until all your numbers display the same, then decrease until you have the required number.

Text format

Text is automatically aligned to the left of the cell. The exercise will usually require you to right align specified titles, those over columns of numbers. Text alignment and formatting works with the same buttons as in word processing. Select the headings and click on the Align Right button.

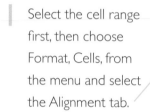

Align Right

You can, however, experiment with the alignment options to enhance the spreadsheet for your own purposes.

1   Select the cell range first, then choose Format, Cells, from the menu and select the Alignment tab.

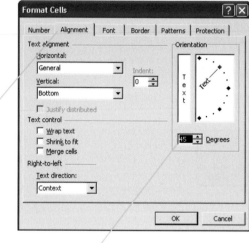

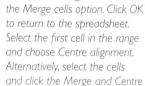
2   You will see a variety of text alignment options, including one to change the orientation of the text. These text headings are set at 45 degrees.

Garden Centre	Plants	Hardware	Catering	Sales	Area	Sales per Hectare
Englemere	4122	4560	1255	9937	1.75	5678.285714

3   You can use the Text wrap button to double stack column titles.

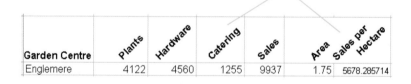

Text control
☑ Wrap text
☐ Shrink to fit
☐ Merge cells

Garden Centre	Plants	Hardware	Catering	Sales	Area	Sales per Hectare

Borders and shading

1 To create a border around a cell or range of cells, first select the cells.

2 The Borders button on the toolbar gives quick access to the range of border options. You can select one or several sides, an outside border, or a full grid. The toolbar button displays the latest selection used.

3 For the full range of options, including selecting line thickness, you must use the Menu and select Format, Cells and the Borders tab.

4 First select the Line Style. You can then choose from the Presets of None, or Outline and/or Inside. Alternatively, select a side or sides by clicking inside the Preview pane, or by using the buttons around it. The buttons are toggles, click to select, click to deselect. Click OK to return to the spreadsheet.

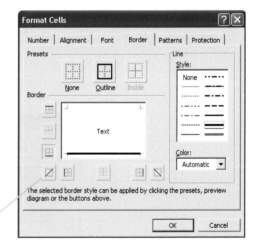

5 Select the Patterns tab to choose an option to fill the cells with colour or pattern. If you do shade the cells, it's a good idea to stay with paler colours, to avoid obscuring the contents.

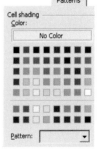

Headers and footers

You can access the Headers and Footers window by selecting Print Preview and Setup.

1 To create Headers and Footers to your document, select File, Page Setup and the Headers and Footers tab.

Headers and Footers that have been created previously can be viewed and selected by clicking on the drop down arrow on the Header or Footer bar.

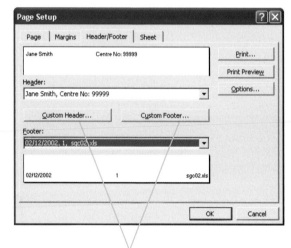

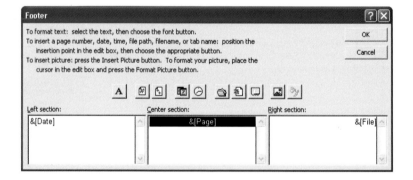

2 Click on the Custom Header or Custom Footer button.

3 The Header or Footer area is divided into three sections and each section or edit box is treated independently.

4 For plain text, such as your name or centre number, you can just click in a box and type.

Using Autotext means that file names, dates and page numbers get updated automatically.

Autotext

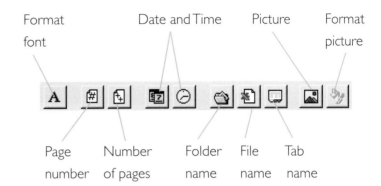

Format font   Date and Time   Picture   Format picture

Page number   Number of pages   Folder name   File name   Tab name

Check that the date format is in UK: dd/mm/yyyy.

The Header and Footer toolbar provides autotext buttons. Click in each section of the Header or Footer in turn and select the required item. You will only see symbols, such as &[File] or &[Page].

Column/row headings and gridlines

Printing column and row headings lets you check your formulae in hard copy to ensure that you reference the correct cells.

Select File, Page Setup and the Sheet tab to access special features for printing. You can select an area to print, Print titles (column and row labels which will be repeated on each page), Gridlines or Row and column headings (ABC, 123).

2 Be sure to use Print Preview before actually printing to confirm you have the required details and everything displays correctly.

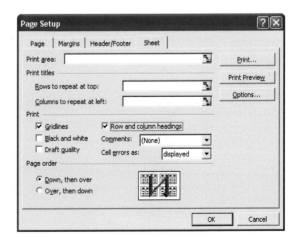

Printing spreadsheets

You should always use the Print Preview facility with spreadsheets. It can save time, paper and frustration.

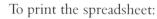

To print the spreadsheet:

1 Click on File, Print Preview, or select the Print Preview button. The Preview window has its own toolbar. The Previous and Next buttons allow you to scroll through the pages. The Zoom or magnifying glass switch between full page or detail view.

Use the Close button on the toolbar to return to the spreadsheet.

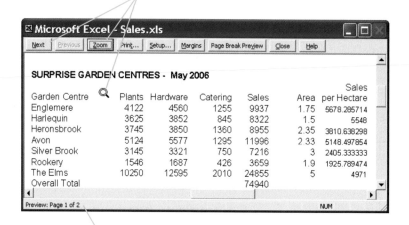

2 The Status bar indicates that the print will take two pages. To change the paper orientation, which may reduce the printout to just one page, select the Setup button and choose Landscape. Click on OK to return to the Preview window to view the result.

Most spreadsheet printouts require landscape orientation.

Only use the Fit to: option to achieve a slight reduction in size, unless of course the exercise specifies that you print on one page. Practically speaking, it is often better to print on two pages. You must be able to see all the data, so check the columns on your finished printout to make sure they are wide enough, especially when printing formulae.

3 If specified by the exercise, select Fit to: and reduce the print to one page.

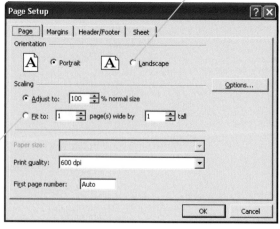

Print Formulae

It is essential to provide a printout of formulae used in the spreadsheet. Normally, formulae is only visible in the Formula bar, and the result of the calculation is shown in the cells. To view formulae used in the spreadsheet:

1 Select Tools, Options, and the View tab.

2 Tick the box for Formulas and click OK.

3 When you return to the spreadsheet view you will see the formulae in the spreadsheet cells. In this view the alignment and formatting of numbers

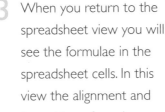

have been dropped. You do not need to worry about this. This print is required to demonstrate that formulae are used, and copied correctly.

Use the easy shortcut to view formulae: hold down the Ctrl key and press ¬ (the key above the Tab key). This toggles you in and out of formulae view.

OCR use the term formulae, Microsoft use the more mundane formulas.

You must check the column widths and ensure that all formulae are displayed in full, including trailing brackets – this doesn't always happen automatically. You don't need to make any other changes.

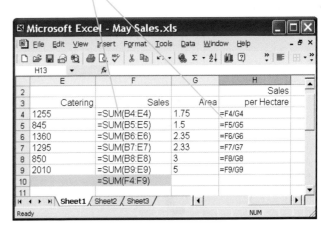

You can select an area of the spreadsheet, and in the Print dialog box choose to print Selection.

4 Select Print Preview and check the printout as before. Click the Print button to invoke the Print dialog box and select OK.

Charts

Each type of graph or chart has its own particular strengths for illustrating data.

Charting data is a very good way to highlight particular trends or patterns. It makes comparison of data much simpler, and can make the data easier to explain and understand. Charts provide an important visual element to reports, helping to make them more interesting and professional.

 Column chart – compares one or more types of data on a vertical axis, accepted by New CLAiT as a bar chart

 Bar chart – compares one or more types of data on a horizontal axis

The exercise will tell you which chart to use, so you just need to follow instructions.

 Line graph – shows up and down movement and trend over time

 Pie chart – compares relative values of parts to a whole item or collection

These are most of the standard graphs offered in Excel. Others include Radar, Cylinder, Cone and Pyramid. There are also a multitude of Custom Types provided in the Chart Wizard.

 XY Scatter graph – shows the relationship between two related data types

 Area graph – illustrates the relative importance of values over time

 Doughnut chart – like a pie chart, but may contain more than one series

 Stock chart – with both line and column entries, this is designed especially to highlight stock market trends

Parts of a chart

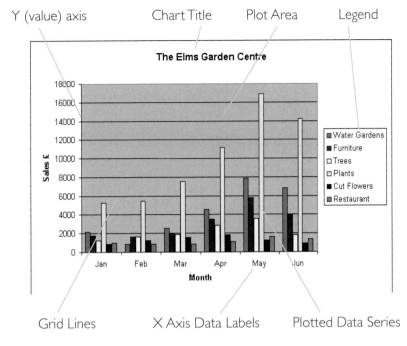

Y (value) axis   Chart Title   Plot Area   Legend

Grid Lines   X Axis Data Labels   Plotted Data Series

The plotted figures are the data series. Excel will use the row labels as the series names.

Chart title	–	will be keyed in as part of the exercise
Plot area	–	the background to the columns or lines
Legend	–	table identifying each column or data series
X axis	–	the identifying axis with data labels
Y axis	–	shows the value or quantity
Grid lines	–	indicate stages or values at regular intervals
Axis labels	–	will be keyed in as part of the exercise

The Chart data

You will be provided with a spreadsheet containing the necessary data. Creating graphs from a datasheet works best when there are no blank columns or rows in the data, so if there are any, it's a good idea to delete them before you start.

You can chart just a subset of the rows and columns of your data.

	A	B	C	D	E	F	G
1	The Elms Garden Centre						
2	Department	Jan	Feb	Mar	Apr	May	Jun
3	Water Gardens	2120	825	2533	4528	7856	6850
4	Furniture	1750	1625	1935	3535	5785	3995
5	Trees	1250	1655	1857	2845	3545	1835
6	Plants	5255	5480	7535	11185	16882	14228
7	Cut Flowers	874	1255	1565	1796	1229	888
8	Restaurant	950	873	820	1120	1653	1388

Create a pie chart

It's a good idea to save your datasheet with a different file name, right at the beginning. Then, if you inadvertently change any data, you can go back to the original.

1 Select the data you wish to graph. You can include the title, and the row and column headings. Remember, cell A1 contains all the title text and is the first selected cell in the range, so remains white.

	A	B	C	D
1	The Elms Garden Centre			
2	Department	Jan	Feb	Mar
3	Water Gardens	2120	825	2533
4	Furniture	1750	1625	1935
5	Trees	1250	1655	1857
6	Plants	5255	5480	7535
7	Cut Flowers	874	1255	1565
8	Restaurant	950	873	820

You should select the data that you want to graph, before you start the Chart Wizard. You can re-select at Step 2 of the Wizard, but it is easier and quicker to do it first.

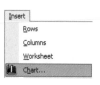

2 Select Insert, Chart from the menu bar, to start the Chart Wizard or click on the Chart Wizard on the toolbar.

3 The Chart Wizard takes you through four steps to create the chart. Step 1 displays a dialog box with a list of chart types in the left pane, and a preview window on the right.

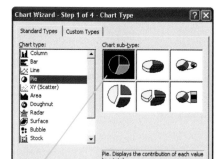

You can select the Custom tab, and Black and White Pie, if you don't have a colour printer. See page 95 for other alternatives.

4 Select Pie from the left pane. In the Preview pane, the sample in black is the default choice.

At this point you can see that the Wizard has picked up the chart title, and the segment labels. If some details are missing, you should be able to see them later in the Wizard, or on the finished chart.

5 Use the Press and Hold facility to view a sample of your data in the chosen chart style.

6 Select Next to move to the next step.

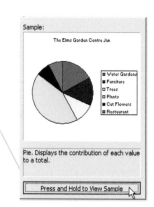

Create a pie chart – step 2

1 Step two of the Wizard highlights with a flashing dotted line, the data range you had previously selected.

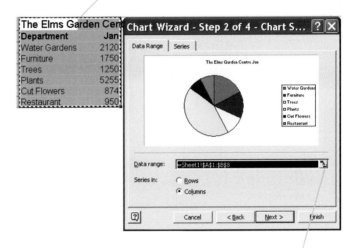

The Collapse Dialog button is also used with the Formula Function in Excel, as you see on page 71.

2 If necessary, re-select the data range. Click on the Collapse dialog button. This reduces this window to just a bar, allowing you to view the selected data range, and change it if necessary. Click again on the button to re-display the window.

The Series tab will be examined in greater detail, later in the unit. See page 93.

3 The Series tab shows where the Wizard is getting the information. It is using Sheet 1, cells B1 and B2 for the specific name, and B3 to B8 for the values.

4 The Category labels, Water Gardens, Furniture, Trees etc. are found on Sheet 1, cells A3 to A8. Excel applied the correct labels because the data range was pre-selected.

Create a pie chart – step 3

1. This next step allows you to add the required details to the chart. The Chart title has been created from information on the spreadsheet. You can amend it now if it is not as specified in the exercise.

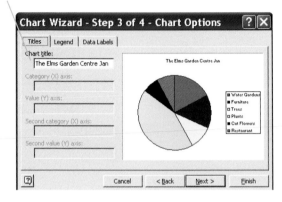

Note that at any point in the Charting process you can cancel, or go backwards. You can also select Finish, but this does skip two stages that are designed to help with the finer details of the chart.

2. The Wizard has automatically generated a legend. For a pie chart, the legend may not be the best way to identify the different sectors. Select the Legend tab, and remove the tick.

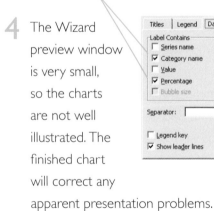

In a coloured pie chart, and specifically with a colour printed pie chart, the legend will identify the various sectors. However, with a black and white print, the differences are not so obvious. See page 95 for how to change the way the sectors are displayed.

3. Select the Data Labels tab and view the effects of selecting the different options offered. The best combination for the CLAiT exercise is the Category name and Percentage or Value. Using the Category name ensures that there is no confusion over sector identity on the finished print.

4. The Wizard preview window is very small, so the charts are not well illustrated. The finished chart will correct any apparent presentation problems.

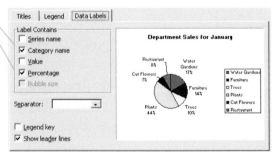

Create a pie chart – step 4

If you don't supply a name for the new sheet, it will be called Chart 1, or Chart 2 etc.

To delete the chart when it is an object on the sheet, select it and press the Delete keyboard key.

The chart has its own frame, and can be re-sized and moved the same as any picture or image frame. For more on frames see Unit 4, e-Publication Creation.

Check your finished graph to ensure that you have not included blank cells. These will show as a thin line and a 0% allocation. Also make sure that any headings or axes entries are spelled correctly.

The last step in the Wizard is to select how to view the chart, on its own sheet or as an object on the data sheet. The New CLAiT exercise will specify the presentation. Supply a name for the chart sheet, to help identify it and click Finish. To review the underlying data, select the Sheet tab. Any changes made to the data will be reflected in the chart.

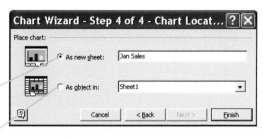

The default on Step 4 is to view the chart as an embedded object in the current sheet, with the data source identified, as shown.

	A	B	C	D	E	F	G	H
1	The Elms Garden Centre							
2	Department	Jan	Feb	Mar	Apr	May	Jun	
3	Water Gardens	2120	825	2533	4528	7856	6850	
4	Furniture	1750						
5	Trees	1250						
6	Plants	5255						
7	Cut Flowers	874						
8	Restaurant	950						
9								
10								
11								
12								
13								
14								
15								
16								

Department Sales for January

Restaurant 8%
Water Gardens 17%
Cut Flowers 7%
Furniture 14%
Plants 44%
Trees 10%

To change the chart from its own sheet or as Object in, select Chart, Location. (The chart must be selected to see Chart on the toolbar.) This invokes the dialog box as shown above.

Bar/column chart

The data that you are using for all the graphs is usually one range of consecutive cells. Make sure that you select that part of the range that you want to use, each time you start a new graph.

For the purposes of the New CLAiT course, the bar and column chart formats are equally acceptable. Microsoft prefers to use the term Bar for horizontal columns, and Column for vertical. To create a bar or column chart:

1. Select your data and click on the Chart Wizard. Select Column or Bar. In either case, one example will be the default, and it's generally advisable to stay with the default.

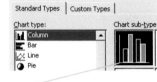

2. On Step 2 the Wizard has generated a scale. At this point you must accept the upper and lower ranges and must wait until the chart is finished. See page 92 for how to change the scale.

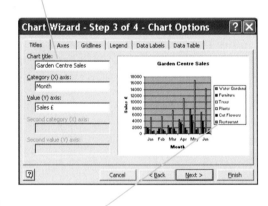

The bar or column graph shows a discrete or specific value, usually at a point in time. It is also used for comparing sets of data values.

3. Step 3 allows you to add a title and X and Y axis labels. For this chart you must enter the title as Excel does not do it for you. As you type into the relevant boxes, the information will be added to the preview.

4. This step allows you to modify the position of the legend, or remove it. However, unlike the pie chart, the legend on this graph is essential.

5. Click Next to move to the final step, select a location and Finish.

Line graph

1 The line graph is created in the same way as the bar and column charts. Select the appropriate data, start the Chart Wizard and follow all the steps through to completion.

2 To change the lines on the line graph to make them more significant, select the line itself. Then click with the right mouse button to bring up the Context menu.

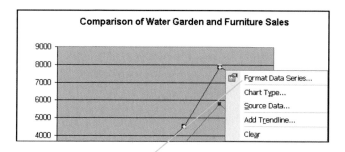

3 Select Format Data Series. This dialog box allows you to change the line colour, style and thickness of the line. You will need to perform this action for each line in the chart.

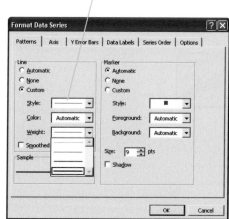

4 To change the grey background, position the mouse in the Plot Area and click with the right mouse button. From the Context menu select Format Plot Area.

5 To change the Plot Area to white, click on the white square and select OK.

Editing charts

Each part of a chart is a separate entity that can be edited, moved and changed independently. When you click to select any part of the chart you will see its frame.

When the Chart sheet is the active sheet, you will see Chart appear on the Menu bar, providing access to the Chart options and functions.

1 To add a chart title or axis labels, click in the chart to activate it, and from the Menu bar select Chart, Chart Options. This displays the window available on Step 3 of the Wizard, see page 86. You can now add or amend the title and labels.

Chart
Chart Type...
Source Data...
Chart Options...
Location...
¥

2 An easy way to change the title or labels, is to

Comparison of Water Garden and Furniture Sales

click on the item twice. The first click selects the item, the second positions the cursor, ready for you to use the normal editing tools.

3 To edit the actual figures that are plotted, return to the original data, and make the amendments there. The plotted graph will automatically change to reflect the new figures.

You can use the Context menu, invoked by the right mouse button, for most of these items.

4 To change the data range that is plotted, select the chart and from the Menu choose Chart, Source data. This displays the dialog box, as shown in Step 2 of the Wizard, see page 85. Use the Collapse dialog button to minimise the window, and re-select the range.

For details on how to change the chart location see page 87.

5 Note that in re-selecting the data range, the legend has changed to identify the lines as Series 1 and 2. See page 93 for how to correct.

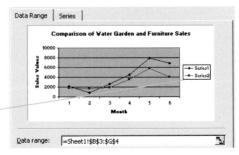

The chart toolbar

The chart toolbar provides some useful facilities, and is a quick way to access some of the most used functions.

To view the chart toolbar:

1 Select View, Toolbars, and the Chart toolbar.

2 The toolbar may appear on its own line under the Standard or Formatting toolbar, or it may float on the screen.

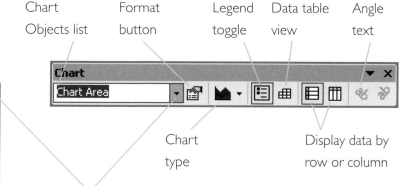

Chart Objects list • Format button • Legend toggle • Data table view • Angle text

Chart type • Display data by row or column

3 The Chart Objects list displays the name of the part of the chart selected. To format any part, select from the drop-down list and click on the Format button.

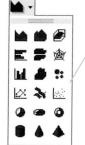

4 The Chart type can be changed by selecting from a series of styles displayed on the Chart type button.

5 The Legend and Data table options are both toggle switches, so you can see the chart with and without these additions.

6 You can use the Display data by row or column buttons to view the other way to present the data, if the default does not suit you.

Amend the scale

The Y axis is the value axis, in other words, it shows the number sold, or the cost of sales, or the value of sales. The Y axis on the Bar chart is horizontal, and on the Column chart it is vertical.

The scale measurements are automatically created by Excel, based on the information in the spreadsheet. In the CLAiT exercise you will be required to display the scale with a particular maximum and minimum.

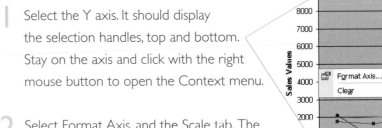

1 Select the Y axis. It should display the selection handles, top and bottom. Stay on the axis and click with the right mouse button to open the Context menu.

Check that the whole of the chart area is not selected. The selection handles should only appear on the Y axis. When the mouse pointer is on the correct axis, it will display the Value Axis message.

2 Select Format Axis, and the Scale tab. The CLAiT exercise will tell you what to set as the minimum and maximum.

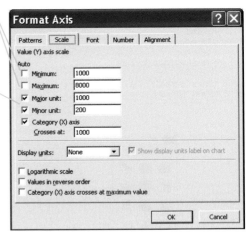

3 Check the Major and Minor unit. Problems arise when the difference between the Minimum and Maximum is not divisible by the Major unit. This may change the point at which the axes cross, or cause a different maximum to be used from that specified.

When you change the font size, style or alignment, it only applies to the selected axis. Select the other axis and follow the same procedure.

4 Use this dialog box to change the font size, style and alignment.

Troubleshooting

The Series tab on Step 2 of the Wizard, see page 85, shows where on the spreadsheet the data has been selected, and how it has been used. For creating a simple pie, bar or line chart, you may never need to look at this tab or make any changes to it. There are, however, some circumstances that may arise during the completion of an exercise where amending these details becomes necessary.

The Legend

You may find that when your chart has been created there is no legend, or the legend entry reads Series 1, and/or 2. In order to interpret the Chart, the legend must specify the correct series names.

1 Select the chart, and from the Menu click Chart, Source Data. Click the Series tab, if necessary.

2 The Wizard has used the cell address in the Name box to find the series name, ie

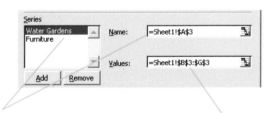

Water Gardens in A3, and the matching values from the adjacent cells on the spreadsheet, B3 to G3.

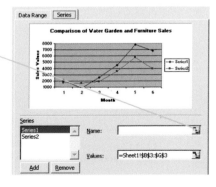

3 If the Series box contains Series 1 instead of a name, click on the Collapse dialog button in the Name box and select the cell on the spreadsheet that contains the appropriate name. You would need to select each series in the list, e.g. Series 2 (Furniture) and perform the same actions again.

There are occasions when data labels are numbers, such as years, part numbers, ages etc. The Wizard will automatically plot these, creating a series entry for them. In plotting the data labels, the Wizard does not use them to assign an identity to the data.

Notice how in the example illustrated here, the Chart Wizard has taken the Department and Years as data to be plotted, shown as a flat red plotted line on the chart. Also, the X axis data labels are missing, and the default values of 1-5 have been inserted.

1 To remove the incorrect series, select Chart, Source Data, and the Series tab.

The Elms Garden Centre						
Department	2001	2002	2003	2004	2005	2006
Water Gardens	2120	825	2533	4528	7856	6850
Furniture	1750	1625	1935	3535	5785	3995

In Format, Cells, there is an option to treat numbers as text. Unfortunately this just changes the alignment, the Chart Wizard will still plot them as numbers.

2 In the Series pane select the entry that is not required and Remove. You will see the effect immediately in the preview pane.

3 These numbers can now be used as the X axis labels. Click the Collapse dialog button to return to the spreadsheet and select them. Again, you should see the effect in the preview pane.

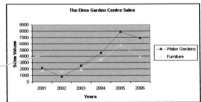

Changing segment display

For a chart to be useable, the data it is illustrating must be clearly identified. Colour monitors make it easy to differentiate between pie chart segments, or lines on a line graph. However, the printed copy may be quite different. Shades of grey or deeper colours may appear alike.

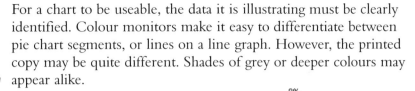

1 To change a segment on a pie chart click on the pie itself, and then click on the particular segment. The first click selects the pie and the second the segment.
Still on the segment, right click and select Format Data Point.

2 From the Format Data Point dialog box select the Fill Effects option, and then the Pattern tab.

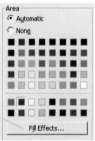

3 Select from the numerous options, remembering to ensure that the final choice clearly identifies the segment.

4 The same process applies to bar and column charts. Select the series you wish to amend. Right click and select Format Data Series.

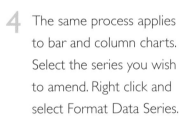

5 The whole series has been selected in this example. If you were to click again on one column, you would select just that one.

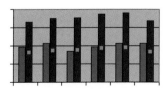

Printing charts

You should save each chart as a separate sheet within the file. It's a good idea to make a second copy of the file, when you have finished.

Printing the charts is a very simple process. For New CLAiT it is usually sufficient to print each chart on a separate page.

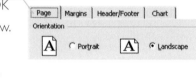

With the chart on the screen, select Print Preview.

If you don't need to change anything, you can just click on Print.

| Next | Previous | Zoom | Print... | Setup... | Margins | Page Break Preview | Close |

If you need to print the supporting data with a chart, save it as an object on the spreadsheet. Alternatively you can use the Data table button on the Chart toolbar to display the table.

2 To change the orientation select Setup and the Page tab. Click OK to return to the Preview window. Click Close on the Preview window to return to the Chart.

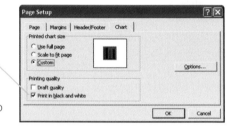

Headers and Footers are added in exactly the same way as for spreadsheets. See page 78.

3 The Chart tab provides more printing options, for example to print in black and white. This is a quick way to change the chart to ensure that the segments are noticeably different when printed.

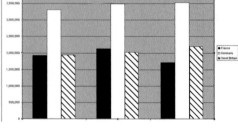

If an embedded chart is selected, it will print as if it were on a separate sheet.

4 To print a reduced size chart, select Custom and OK.

5 You must return to the Chart sheet, not the Preview window, to change the size. Click on the chart to display the selection handles, and drag to resize.

Unit 2 exercise

Scenario

Before you begin the exercise, make a subfolder called Unit 2 in the CLAiT Coursework folder as a storage area to contain your answers.

You are working as an administrative assistant for Surprise Garden Centres. You have been asked to produce a report showing the sales for the garden centres for the month of May.

Task 1

1. Create a new spreadsheet using the data below.

SURPRISE GARDEN CENTRES – May 2006						
GARDEN CENTRE	PLANTS	HARDWARE	CATERING	SALES	AREA	SALES PER HECTARE
ENGLEMERE	4122	4560	1255		1.75	
HARLEQUIN	3625	3852	845		1.5	
HERONSBROOK	3745	3850	1360		2.35	
AVON	5124	5577	1295		2.33	
SILVER BROOK	3145	3321	750		3	
ROOKERY	1546	1687	426		1.9	
THE ELMS	10250	12595	2010		5	
OVERALL TOTAL						

2. Enter your name and centre number into the header area of the spreadsheet.

You are allowed two and a half hours to complete this assignment.

3. Include an automatic file name in the footer area.
4. SALES is calculated by adding together the figures for PLANTS, HARDWARE and CATERING.
   Insert a formula to calculate the SALES for ENGLEMERE.
5. Replicate this formula to show the SALES for all the other garden centres.
6. The OVERALL TOTAL is calculated by adding together all the sales figures. Insert a formula at the bottom of the SALES column to calculate the OVERALL TOTAL.
7. The SALES PER HECTARE figure is calculated by dividing SALES by AREA.

Insert a formula to calculate the SALES PER HECTARE for ENGLEMERE.

8. Replicate this formula for the other centres.
9. Save your spreadsheet with the filename Sales into the Unit 2 subfolder..
10. Print one copy showing the figures, not the formulae. Make sure that all the data is displayed in full.

Task 2

Your manager wants you to make some changes to the report.

1. THE ROOKERY is to be sold. Delete this entire row.
2. Make the following amendments to the spreadsheet:
    a. The HARDWARE figure for AVON should be 4250.
    b. The CATERING figure for SILVERBROOK should be 850.
    c. SILVER BROOK should be spelled SILVERBROOK.
3. Make sure that the SALES and SALES PER HECTARE figures have updated as a result of these changes.

Your manager wants you to format the report.

4. Apply alignment as follows:
    a. The column heading GARDEN CENTRES and all the row labels should be left aligned.
    b. The other column headings (e.g. PLANTS) should be right aligned.
    c. All numeric data should be right aligned.
5. Format the data.
    a. The figures for PLANTS, HARDWARE and CATERING should be in integer format (zero decimal places).
    b. The figures for SALES, and AREA should be displayed to two decimal places.
    c. The SALES PER HECTARE data only should be displayed with a £ sign and two decimal places.

6. Save the spreadsheet as Sales1.

7. Print a copy of the spreadsheet.

Task 3

It has been decided to include the figures for the Outlet franchises.

1. Insert a column headed OUTLETS between CENTRES and PLANTS.

2. The heading should be right aligned. The figures should be right aligned and displayed in Integer format (zero decimal places.)

3. Starting with ENGLEMERE and ending with THE ELMS the figures

   are:
ENGLEMERE	9910
HARLEQUIN	4555
HERONSBROOK	6858
AVON	10150
SILVERBROOK	7700
THE ELMS	15800

4. Make sure that the figures for SALES and SALES PER HECTARE are updated to include OUTLETS.

5. Save your spreadsheet with the filename May Sales. Make sure that the automatic file name has been updated.

6. Print a copy showing figures, not formulae. Make sure that all data is displayed in full.

7. Print the spreadsheet on one page in landscape layout, with the formulae showing. Make sure that all formulae are displayed in full.

8. Include the column heading and row headings (A,B,C and 1,2,3) and gridlines on the printout.

Task 4

Your manager has asked you to make certain changes.

1. Format the OVERALL TOTAL row with a light green fill colour.

2. Format the SALES column with the same fill colour.

3. Put a border around the SALES Per HECTARE column.

4.   Save the file with the name May Sales 1.

5.   Print the spreadsheet with the figures showing. Make sure that all figures are displayed.

Task 5

You have been asked to produce some reports in graph format relating to the Elms Garden Centre.

To complete this part of the exercise you will need the file The Elms.xls from the NC2006data folder. Copy it into Unit 2 subfolder in CLAiT Coursework. See page 253 for downloading the files from the In Easy Steps web site.

1.   Open the data file The Elms.xls, which contains data on sales by various departments for January to June.

2.   Create a pie chart to display the January data for all departments.

3.   Title the chart Department Sales for January 2006.

4.   Each sector must be easily identifiable.

5.   Each sector must be clearly labelled with the department name and either the value or percentage.

6.   In the header area enter your name, and an automatic file name.

7.   Save the file with the name The Elms Graphs.

8.   Print a copy of the chart in Landscape layout, on one page.

Task 6

The manager needs to evaluate sales values for Water Gardens and Furniture.

When you have finished this exercise you should have the following files and printouts:
Sales
Sales 1
May Sales (figures)
May Sales (formulae)
May Sales 1
The Elms Graphs (pie chart)
The Elms Graphs (line graph)

1.   Create a line graph comparing the data for Water Gardens and Furniture sales for January to June.

2.   Display the months along the x-axis.

3.   Set the y-axis range from 1000 to 8000

4.   Title the graph Comparison of Water Garden and Furniture Sales.

5.   Label the x-axis Months and the y-axis Sales Values.

6.   Use a legend to identify each line. Make sure that each line can be easily identified.

7.   Save the file and print a copy of the line graph in portrait layout with supporting data.

Database Manipulation

This unit introduces managing databases using Microsoft Access. It includes adding, amending and deleting entries. It covers how to sort the database table, create search queries and print reports. It also covers database table creation.

Covers

The database | 102

Start Access | 103

The main database window | 104

Tables | 105

Editing the table | 107

Find and replace | 108

Sort | 109

Filters | 110

Queries | 111

Create a query | 112

Printing tables and queries | 114

Reports | 115

Close the database | 119

Create your own table | 120

Unit 3 exercise | 122

Unit Three

The database

A database is simply information organised in a logical and structured way. An address book, calendar or the telephone directory are examples of simple databases that you use every day.

A computerised database offers great flexibility. It allows you to add data, to edit or make changes to individual items promptly and to delete redundant data. It means you can manipulate the information, sort and find specific information quickly and easily.

Microsoft Excel

You could use a spreadsheet, such as Excel, to manage the database. It has many of the required functions. You can sort data easily, and search for specific

data using the Filter function – indeed for a small database it may be the best choice, but it does have drawbacks. The spreadsheet is loaded into memory and works in memory. This may cause problems with large amounts of data. The spreadsheet format is not ideally suited to managing search or query results, especially when you have multiple queries. You are also susceptible to potential loss or corruption of data.

Microsoft Access

Access is a database program that is designed to work with large volumes of data. It writes the data to disk automatically as you work, so it is less likely to lose data. It allows you to perform all standard database activities in a controlled manner. It has tools and functions to manage input, editing, sorting and reports on the data. All these actions are carried out within the database file.

This method of storing data along with the links between data elements is known as relational database, and the type of software that supports it is known as a relational database management system (RDBMS).

It allows you to input information into separate tables in the same database and link the tables. For example, in an employment database you could have three tables. One may contain personal information, such as address, marital status etc; one may have employment data such as payroll number, date started, NI number; and the third, assigned company car details. When you need information about an individual employee, you can link the tables together.

Start Access

To start Access, select Start, All Programs, Microsoft Access.

When you open Access, you are presented with a blank Database window and the Task Pane.

Title bar

Menu bar

Toolbars

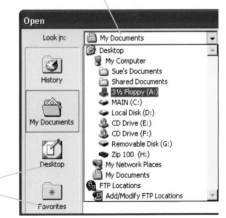

Until you create or open a database, only the New, Open and Search buttons are available. The remainder are inactive.

You will be given a database to work with for the New CLAiT exercises, so you do not have to create one. You may be told where to find the database file, or you can use the Search facility provided by Windows. To locate the file if it is not already listed on the Task Pane:

Access uses the file extension .mdb.

1 Select More files. Access will be configured to look automatically in My Documents on the main C: drive. If the file is there, just select it and click Open or double click it.

See page 120 if you wish to create your own database table.

2 If the file is in a different location, click the down arrow next to My Documents in the Look in bar, and navigate the drives and folders.

3 These icons present shortcuts to various locations on the computer.

You can use File, Open, if the Task Pane is not available.

4 When you open the file, it displays the main Database window.

The main database window

The database file always opens as a small window rather than full screen. It's a good idea to maximise it when you open a table or query.

The main database window presents a series of objects or functions for you to use.

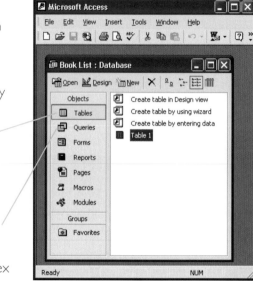

1 Tables. These contain the basic data of the database. In this database there is only one table and it is currently selected.

You are only expected to use Tables, Queries and Reports in the New CLAiT course.

2 Queries. These are saved searches. You can look for specific information in the database, use complex criteria and save it for later re-use.

All the objects for a particular database are stored in a single Access database file.

3 Forms. You can create custom forms for data input. Using forms can speed up data entry by filling in standard fields, such as today's date, department, etc, or by limiting the input to just some of the fields in the data table.

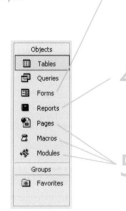

4 Reports. You can print data tables or queries in table format. Reports allow you to present the data in more readable or attractive way. You can use reports to create summary documents.

5 Pages are a means of sharing Access data across a network. Macros and Modules are complex features used by database programmers to create and run programs to perform a series of repetitive tasks. They use Visual Basic programming language.

Tables

The database table has a defined structure. Information is divided firstly into records. A record is all the information about an individual entry in the list, so for example in the telephone directory a record is name, initials, address, town and phone number for one person.

Within each record, the data is divided into fields.

FIELD 1 Surname	FIELD 2 Initials	FIELD 3 Address	FIELD 4 Town	FIELD 5 Phone No
Smith	J	1 The Highway	Anytown	01234-456789
Williams	J	2 London Road	Newtown	01222-333333

The type of information contained within each field is categorised. There are ten data types:

Text	text or combination of text and numbers
Memo	longer text entries
Number	numbers only, with or without decimals
Date/Time	date format 25/06/07 or 25-Jun-07
Currency	with £ or Euro
Autonumber	system generated to identify each record
Yes/No	logical, true/false, on/off
OLE Object	linked to an object elsewhere on PC
Hyperlink	linked to an object on a network
Lookup Wizard	create a link to another table

The data tables that you will use should only contain text, number, currency and date fields.

When the database table is created, the content of each field is assessed to determine the data type. By assigning each field a data type, a certain level of validation is achieved, for example, you cannot type text into a number field. When you use the tables created for you in the CLAiT exercises the data type is already set.

You must have the Tables tab selected to see the list of tables.

To open the table:

Select the table and double click the icon next to the table name (or press the Open button).

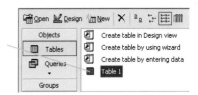

...cont'd

The tables you are given for practice may not have the ID autonumber field. It is recommended database practice to have one, but not essential. It will not affect any activities in the database at New CLAiT level.

The database table is presented in datasheet view, the layout is very similar to a spreadsheet. Each row contains one record and each record is divided into fields. The column headings show the field names.

Autonumber Field   Date Field   Currency Field

Design view button

Number of records in database

Current record

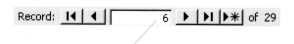

ID	NAME	TYPE	COLOUR	SEASON	HEIGHT (CMS)	AVAILABLE	PRICE	In Stock
1	CAMPANULA	PERENNIAL	WHITE	SPRING	35	01/03/2007	£1.50	☑
2	HOSTA	PERENNIAL	GREY	SUMMER	15	20/03/2007	£3.65	☑
3	LAVATERA	SHRUB	PINK	SUMMER	150	25/04/2006	£5.99	☑
4	OXALIS	PERENNIAL	PINK	WINTER	15	01/10/2006	£2.50	☑
5	SEDUM	PERENNIAL	RED	AUTUMN	40	02/04/2007	£1.75	☐
6	LILIUM	BULB	CREAM	SUMMER	100	20/03/2007	£2.75	☑

Record: 16 of 16

Datasheet View   NUM

Text   Number   Yes/No
Field   Field   Field

Access saves any data changes to disk automatically, without asking for confirmation. Make sure that you do not change any data inadvertently.

2 You can move around the table using the scroll bars, the arrow keys or the Tab key.

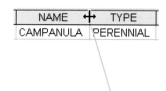

Record: 6 of 29

3 Click in the Record indicator and type a number to go to that record. You can also select first, next in either direction or last.

Change column widths

You may also choose to narrow some columns, thus making more of the table visible at one time.

1 When you open the table, you may need to change some column widths to display all the data.

NAME	TYPE
CAMPANULA	PERENNIAL

You must display all the data in a column. This is a New CLAiT 2006 course requirement.

2 Position the mouse on the divider between the column headings and drag to the desired width, or double click.

Editing the table

Add records

1 Click on the Add records button on the Toolbar. This positions the cursor at the end of the table. Just press Enter to skip the ID field (if present) as Access will enter a number for you, and input the data.

2 As you enter the data, it is automatically written to disk. You do not have to save it.

Amend records

1 Just position the cursor on the data you wish to edit and retype.

2 The amendments are saved automatically.

Delete records

1 Select the record by clicking on the row heading.

13	BEGONIA	BULB	YELLOW
14	CANNA	BULB	BRONZE
15	VIBURNUM	SHRUB	PINK

2 Click on the Delete record button on the Toolbar, or press the delete key. You will be warned that the deletion is permanent.

3 You can delete a block of records. Select the first record, press and hold the Shift key, then click the last record of the block.

Find and replace

The Find facility is just a subset of Find and Replace, and can be used in the same way.

The Find and replace facility is used to update fields efficiently, especially when you need to replace the same data in many records.

1   Position your cursor in the column you are going to search. Select the Find button, or choose Edit, Replace from the menu.

2   Click the Replace tab to bring it to the front if necessary. Type in the data to Find, press tab and type in the Replace With data.

Match allows you to choose the whole field, or part of a field.

Leave Match Case unselected to look for all word forms, uppercase and lowercase.

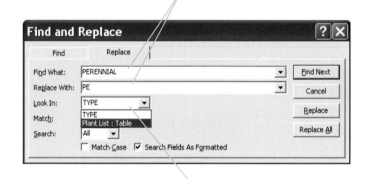

3   The Look In box allows you to limit the search to the current field, the quicker option, or to search the whole table. Search All means the whole column, rather than just from the cursor position.

It is better to restrict the Search to the one field, rather than search the whole table, so you don't get any unexpected results.

4   When you have chosen your options, select Find Next. The cursor moves to the next instance of the search item. To leave this instance, you can select Find Next again.

5   When you select Replace, the item is replaced and the cursor moves automatically to the next instance. Only select Replace All when you have replaced a few and are happy that the facility is working the way you expect.

Replacing data cannot be Undone, since the changes are written to disk.

Sort

The Access table has the Standard toolbar with some new buttons.

Sort Ascending/Descending

Filter by Selection/Form Remove Filter

The sort facility works with numbers, dates, and logical fields as well as text. To sort the table:

1 Position the cursor anywhere in the column you wish to use as the primary sort key. Click on the A to Z to sort in ascending order. The Z to A is reverse sort order, which can be useful with numbers, sorting largest to smallest.

2 When you close the table, you will be asked if you wish to change the design. This relates simply to the re-sorted order of the table.

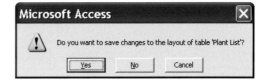

3 Click Yes if you wish to retain the order. However, there is very little advantage in saving the new order, as each time you use the table, you are likely to need to sort it again, either to incorporate new records or to use a different sorting field.

4 You cannot save the table under another name, though you can do so with other database objects.

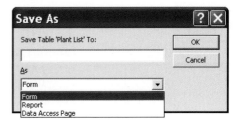

Filters

Criteria are used to identify which particular records you want to choose.

Filters on the database table allow you to select and search for data dynamically. The filter only displays data that matches your selected criteria. The toolbar provides two filters, Filter by Selection and Filter by Form.

To Filter by Selection:

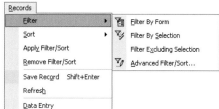

1 Position your cursor in the field which contains your criteria.

2 Select Records, Filter, and Filter by Selection, or you can use the button on the toolbar.

You can print the selected records. Just click on the Print button.

3 The effect is to remove from view all records that do not match the data in the selected field.

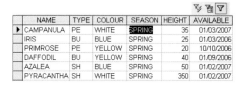

When you apply a filter, you can still see all the information on each record. To see just certain fields in the result, you must use a Query.

4 To remove the filter, and see the complete datasheet once again, click the Remove Filter button, or select Records, Remove Filter/Sort.

The Filter by Form facility allows you to select on more than one criteria. It provides a structured form with drop-down lists for you to select fields and data values to define your criteria. To activate the selection criteria, click on Apply filter. Click Close to return to the table.

Using Filter by Form is not recommended for queries in the New CLAiT course.

Although Filter by Form remembers the filter criteria, you cannot save the search or results, or set any parameters on the search. For all of these activities you have to use an Access query.

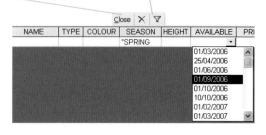

Queries

The Queries facility allows you to:

- Search for records that match one or more criteria
- View selected fields in the result
- Save the query for re-use

Criteria can use complex relationships between fields in a record but for New CLAiT we only need the following types of criteria:

- Matching text values in a field
- Comparing number or date values

To compare use the following notation:

<	Less than
>	Greater than
<=	Less than or equal to
>=	Greater than or equal to

To start a query and select the table:

It's a good idea to start off using the Design View method. You could use the Wizard to create the query, but it only helps you to select the fields, any more complex design features you must create yourself.

1 Select the Queries tab from the main database window.

2 Select Create query in Design view, and click on the Open button.

If we had several related tables in the database file, we could select more than one table at this point. We could create a query that requested information from several tables and brought the information together in one view. This is using Access as a relational database.

3 This displays the Show Table window. This window allows you to choose which table to use in the query. There is only one, already highlighted, so just click Add and then Close.

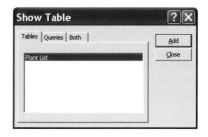

Create a query

1 When you select Add (see page 111) you will find the table appears in the top panel of the Query 1 window. It is provided to enable you to view and select the fields you want in your query.

2 To select the fields, you can double click the required field in the Table window, one at a time. This puts the field into the first and next empty column.

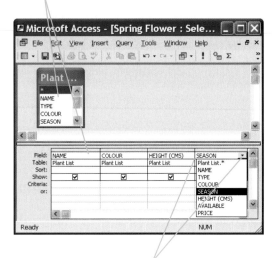

Avoid double clicking to insert a field into a column that is not visible, it looks like nothing has happened and you may end up with the same field selected twice.

3 Alternatively, click in the Field row, and select from the drop-down list. This is the easiest way to select fields if you need more than can be displayed at one time.

Build your query one step at a time. Select your fields, then run the query (see page 113). Return to the design and add one criterion, and run the query again. Return to the design and add another criterion if required, and so on. If at some point your query fails, then you know which step caused the problem.

4 Enter your criteria into the appropriate columns. The criteria illustrated are Spring for Season and less than £4.00 for price. Note that Access inserts the "" around Spring to indicate a text entry, and that although Price is a currency field, you must not type the £ sign, or the query will not work correctly.

Field:	NAME	SEASON	PRICE
Table:	Plant List	Plant List	Plant List
Sort:			
Show:	☑	☑	☐
Criteria:		"Spring"	<4
or:			

The CLAiT exercise will require you to use a criterion to select records, but not display that particular field when you run the query. For example, it may ask you to select on Price, but not require you to display the price in the resulting table.

5 Run the query with the field included to check that the criteria has worked as expected, then return to the design view and de-select the Show box. It will not now display in the result.

Field:	NAME	COLOUR	SEASON	PRICE
Table:	Plant List	Plant List	Plant List	Plant List
Sort:				
Show:	Ascending	☑	☑	☐
Criteria:	Descending			<4
or:	(not sorted)			

6 You may be required to present the results in a particular order. Select from the drop-down list in the appropriate column.

If you add more data to the original table, the next time you run the query new matching data will be added to the result.

When you have built the query as required, you can select either:

Run the Query   View Datasheet

To return to the Design view select:

To save the query:

You can open or save the query in datasheet view or design view.

7 Select File, Save. Supply the name given in the exercise and click on OK. The query is treated as an internal file in the database file.

You may need to add your name to the query name to identify it as yours if you have to share a printer.

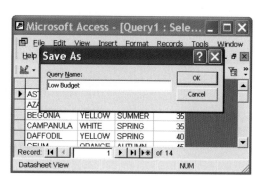

Printing tables and queries

You will need to check every time you print a table or query as Access doesn't remember any previous setup or orientation changes.

Printing tables and queries in the datasheet view is quite straightforward and sufficient for many of the prints required in Unit 3. However, each time you print you must check whether to print in portrait or landscape orientation, to ensure that all the data is visible.

Select your table or query and open it in the datasheet view.

Click on Print Preview. The Status bar informs you if the print will take more than one page.

| Page: |◀| ◀ | 1 | ▶ | ▶| |

It's always easier to read and check a database print if you can manage to get all the columns onto one sheet. To change the page orientation to landscape, select Setup. Click the Page tab to bring it to the fore and select the orientation you require.

| Fit ▼ | Close | Setup |

You can print tables or queries without opening them, if you don't need to change anything. However, you can only access the Setup options through Print Preview, or if the table or query is open.

When you click OK you will return to the Preview window. Click on the Printer button and the document will be printed without need for further intervention.

Always check the column widths on your printout to make sure that all the data is displayed.

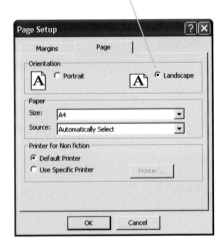

However, when printing tables or queries in this way, there is no header/footer option, or easy method for adding an identifying name or file name. The columns of data often appear too close together and there are no text alignment options. These features are offered in the Access Report function.

Reports

Grouping records allows you to select a field such as Colour in the Plant List database and group all like colours together.

The Summary function means that you can calculate the Sum (total), Average, Maximum and Minimum on any numerical fields in a grouped report.

Reports are used when the presentation of data is important. The Report function in Access allows you to specify text and number alignment, a sort order on up to four fields, a grouping function, and a summary function. The font size, report style and paper orientation are saved in the report setup and the report is then available for repeated use. When the data is amended or updated, the report can be rerun to reflect the changes.

To create a report:

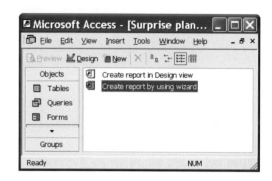

1 Select the Reports tab on the main Database window.

2 Double click on Create report by using wizard.

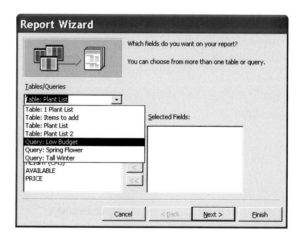

3 With the wizard window open, select from the drop down list, the table or query which is to be used as the basis of the report. You will see the list of fields change to show only those fields used in the selected table or query.

4 Click the single arrow to add individual fields to the report. Click the double arrow to add all fields to the report. Click Next.

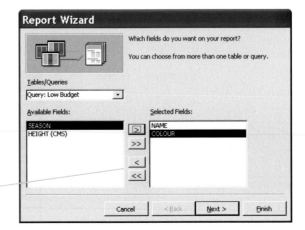

Use the single or double back arrow on these windows to change your selection. Use the Back button to step backwards and make changes to the report.

5 This step allows you to select a grouping level, where like records are listed together. Select the field to be used for grouping in the left pane and click the arrow to transfer it to the preview window. In this example the records will be grouped by Season. Click the Next button to continue.

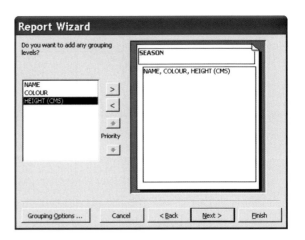

The field that you select for your primary sort order, Name in the example illustrated, will appear first in the report. If you were to choose Height instead, that would be the first column in the report, although currently it is lower on the list. If you specify a grouping level, then a sort order set in a query is over-ridden.

6 In this window you can specify a sort order on up to four fields. Click the down arrow and select the sort field from the list.

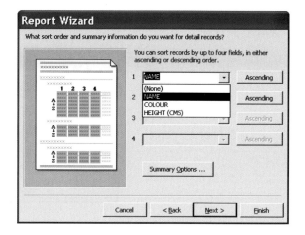

Summary Options are only available if you have specified a grouping level on the previous step.

7 Click Summary Options if you wish to calculate numerical or currency fields. Click Next to continue.

8 In the next two steps choose a layout option, paper orientation and general style for the report. It is worth experimenting with the various layouts at this point as it may save having to adjust the final design. Check the Preview panes to see the different effects.

Note the ticked option in this step to Adjust the field width so that all fields fit on a page. You will need to check the printout to ensure that no columns are truncated and data hidden. This may happen if you have an extra long field or several columns of data.

9 Name the report using that specified in the exercise, accept the default option to preview the report and click Finish.

10 The report opens in a Print preview window. You can scroll to check that no data is obscured or truncated. Switch to Design view to make any necessary changes to the layout.

The report layout consists of a series of text and object frames which are visible in Design view. Using the wizard to create the report establishes the basic layout, including headers, footers and page number. You can then amend it where necessary, working in Design view to move and resize the frames and text boxes. There is more information on working with text frames in Unit 4. (See pages 131-132).

Design view

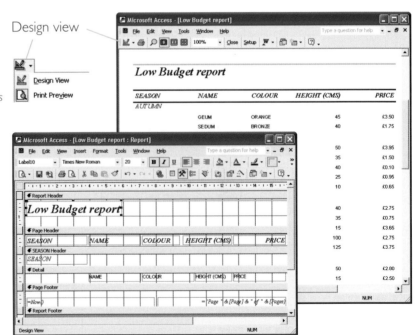

Close the database

When you start the next exercise, you must start a completely new database. Do not create another table within the same one.

By the time you have worked through a complete CLAiT exercise, you will have used a table, created several queries and a report. You will have seen how an Access database contains all these objects, tables, queries, reports etc. within one database file. In Explorer only the .mdb file is visible. You cannot see the tables or queries that have been created and saved within it.

As explained earlier in the unit, you can have more than one table within the database file. However, when you start the next exercise you must start a completely new database. This is because these are separate exercises – you do not wish to create related tables.

Access is designed to prevent confusing tables within a database. When you open a new or second database, it automatically closes the first one.

When you close the database:

1 Close any open tables. Remember, any new or amended data will be saved automatically.

2 Save and close any open queries, if not previously saved. You are saving the design of the query, not the data. If you add more records to your table, the next time you run your query, the results may be different.

3 Close the database file. You will not be prompted to save it, or need to save it.

If you use Excel to create your database, you will need to save the file. Any new or amended data must be saved. In Excel, when you create and run a query, it copies the matching data to an area of the spreadsheet. This will be saved with the spreadsheet, and must be erased before the query can be run again. If you create several queries, managing the resulting output can be quite difficult.

Create your own table

Knowing how to build a database table will be useful, especially if you decide to take a further course. It is quite a simple process, and provides further information on how the database works.

1 Open Access. From the Task Pane select New, Blank database.

2 You are now requested to name the file and save it. Access saves the file first so that it can write data to disk as you type it in. When you have selected the destination folder and supplied the name, click Create.

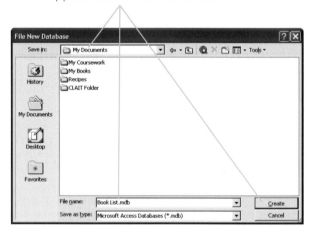

3 The main database window will be displayed with the Tables tab selected.

4 You could use Create table by using wizard. This takes you a step at a time through creating a table using pre-defined templates.

5 However, to maintain complete control over the design process, select Create table in Design view.

6 The Table Design view window presents three columns. In the Field Name column type the text that will become the column heading. Press Enter or tab and move to the Data Type cell.

See page 105 for more detail on data types.

7 In the Data Type cell click the drop-down list and select from the available data types.

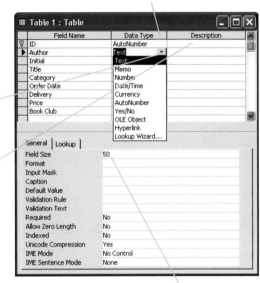

8 The Description area allows for design comments. It does not need to be completed.

9 The Field Properties area lets you select the finer details of how the data can be controlled. For example in a text field, the default field size is 50 characters. In a numeric field you can control the field size, format and decimal places.

Long integer means whole numbers. You must select single or double to use decimal values.

10 When you have completed the design, select File, Save and save the table. You will be prompted to provide a primary key. Click Yes to create the ID field. Close the design view and open in datasheet view to input data. When you open the table you will see the field headings at the top of the table.

Creating a primary key adds an ID field to the database table and allows you to create a relationship between tables in the database.

3. Database Manipulation   121

Unit 3 exercise

If you are using this book for self study, and have downloaded the data files, you'll find the Access file for the Surprise Plants database in the Unit 3 folder.

You are allowed two and a half hours to complete this assignment.

The data file for this exercise can be found in Unit 3 of the NC2006data files, which may be downloaded from the In Easy Steps web site (see page 253). Use the .mdb file for Access 2002 or Access 2000. If you have an older version of Access you can create a new database table following the steps in the file Create_Database.txt.

Scenario

Your Supervisor has asked you to maintain a database of plants and provide reports when required.

Task I

1. Open the Surprise Plants Database. Open the table Plant List. The Plant section manager has decided to add four new plants to the list, and remove from sale one plant that does not grow well in this area.

It's a good idea to make a subfolder called Unit 3 in the CLAiT Coursework folder as a storage area to contain your answer.

2. Create records for the new plants as follows:

   a. The PYRACANTHA is a SHRUB, colour WHITE. It flowers in SPRING at a height of 350 cms. It will be available from 01/02/06, price £7.50.

   b. The VERBASCUM is a PERENNIAL, colour YELLOW. It flowers in SUMMER, grows to 125 cms. It will be available from 25/04/07, price £3.75.

   c. The ASTER is a PERENNIAL, colour BLUE. It flowers in SUMMER, grows to 40 cms. It will be available from 18/04/06, price £2.75.

d. The GEUM is a PERENNIAL, colour ORANGE. It flowers in AUTUMN, grows to 45 cms. It will be available from 01/06/07, price £3.50.

e. It has been decided not to sell the CANNA. Delete the record for CANNA.

3. Close the table and print a copy of the amended table in landscape orientation.

Task 2

Open the table Plant List and make the following changes:

1. Using codes for TYPE would be more efficient. Replace the existing data as follows:
    a. Replace PERENNIAL with PE
    b. Replace SHRUB with SH
    c. Replace BULB with BU

2. Some of the data needs to be amended.
    a. The SEDUM is BRONZE
    b. The PRIMROSE is 10 cms high
    Make these changes and ensure the amended data is saved.

3. Close the table and rename it Plant List 2007.

4. Print the table in landscape orientation, making sure that all data is visible.

Task 3

The Plant Sales Department would like to create a leaflet listing plants for a Spring Garden.

1. Set up the following database query:
    Select all plants that flower in the SPRING
    Sort them into alphabetical order of NAME
    Display only NAME, COLOUR and HEIGHT

2. Save the query as Spring Flowers and print it in table format.

3. The Landscape Department wants a list of winter flowering plants.

Set up the following database query:

Select all plants that bloom in WINTER,

with a height of 50cms or more

Sort the list in ascending order of HEIGHT

Display only NAME, HEIGHT and PRICE

4.   Save the query as Tall Winter Plants and print it in table format.

5.   The Surprise Gardening Club would like to plan a budget garden.

Set up the following database query:

Select all plants that cost less than £4.00

Sort into order of ascending PRICE

Display NAME, COLOUR, SEASON and HEIGHT

6.   Save the query as Budget Plants and print in table format.

Task 4

1.   Create a report using the query Low Budget.

2.   The report must be presented in landscape orientation.

3.   Group the plants by SEASON.

4.   Save the report as Budget Plants Report.

5.   Print the report.

You should have the following prints:

Plant List

Plant List 2007

Spring Flowers

Tall Winter Plants

Budget Plants

Budget Plants Report

e-Publication Creation

In this unit you will learn how to produce simple publications using imported text and image files. It includes managing page layout, moving and resizing text and images, saving and printing.

Covers

Desktop publishing | 126

Start Publisher | 127

The Publisher window | 128

Create a page layout | 129

Templates | 130

Frames and boxes | 131

Import text | 134

Overflow text | 135

Fonts | 136

Text alignment | 137

Import an image file | 138

Image management | 139

Drawing tools | 140

Borders | 141

Final publication layout | 142

Printing publications | 143

Unit 4 exercise | 144

Unit Four

Desktop publishing

Creating a document for publication used to be restricted to the complex skills of the trained typesetter. The mixing of text and pictures of varying styles and sizes into an attractive and acceptable format took time and expertise.

With the advent of the latest computers, and their powerful hardware and sophisticated software, desktop publishing has become available to most computer users. We are able to move and resize objects with just the press of a mouse button and we can view the work in progress and make amendments very easily.

Most of the text editing skills that you learnt in Word can be used in Publisher. Many of the Word Tools, including the Spell Check facility, are also present in Publisher and are accessed and used in a similar fashion.

Word or Publisher

To create a publication, we could use either a word processor, or a desktop publishing program. Word processors today have great functionality. Word, in particular, allows us to work with text and images together on the same page. We can resize and move both text and images. We can draw lines, boxes and other shapes, and we can layer and group objects. In fact, at the beginner level, as required in the New CLAiT course, we could use Word as our desktop publishing program. However, many of these features are secondary functions, harder to access and not so easy to use. The layout and placement of text on the page is controlled by margins, tabs and breaks and offers little flexibility.

A full DTP program, however, provides all these functions and more but with greater ease of use. The Publisher desktop, for example, is larger than a standard sheet of A4 paper, and can be used as a holding area for text and pictures, much as you would use a real desk top. In a desktop publishing package, the text is restricted to the text box, whatever its size, and the text box is treated as an object that can be placed anywhere on the page, moved or resized. Many of Publisher's facilities reflect the finer

It is often better to create paragraphs of text in Word, where you can make editing changes easily. Then copy and paste them into text boxes in Publisher to place them on the page.

details of publishing, such as layout guides and aligning to a grid. There are commercial printing tools, and the facility to create special printouts with colour requisites.

Publisher has a design wizard to help you through the steps involved in creating quite complex publications. It provides templates for you to select from, if you need suggestions or help with designs and layouts, and it can work with varying paper sizes and orientation.

Start Publisher

To open Microsoft Publisher:

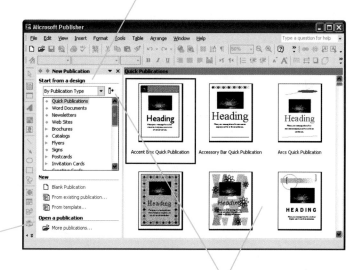

1 Select Start, All programs, Microsoft Publisher. This will open the Publisher window with the New Publisher task pane. If the task pane doesn't appear automatically, select File, New. The task pane displays the publication Wizard design categories.

2 Click the button to display the Publication Gallery, if it's not already visible. This illustrates the publications in the selected category, in this illustration, Quick Publications. Scroll the Preview pane to see the other designs in the category, or click on a different category to view those types of publication.

3 You'd click the down arrow and choose Publications by Design, to select a layout for a fax cover, label, calendar etc. based on a colour and logo concept, providing a consistent house style for your publications.

4 Select the By Blank Publications entry to start with a fresh page.

The Publisher window

1 The Blank Publications gallery shows a variety of page formats and dimensions. Click a page type to start a publication.

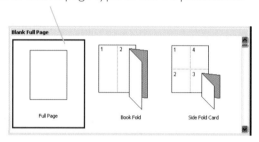

2 This closes the Gallery and reveals a standard sheet of A4 paper, your blank working page. The blue and pink lines are non-printing lines, referred to as layout guides, that indicate the default margins.

Menu bar
Standard toolbar
Objects toolbar
Select Objects
Text Box
Insert Table
Insert Word Art
Picture Frame
Clip Art Frame
Drawing Tools
AutoShapes
Web Page Tools
Design Gallery object
Vertical Ruler
Object Size
Object Position
Page Navigation

Create a page layout

The standard page size for all documents in the UK is A4, paper orientation is normally Portrait, i.e. upright. To change the page orientation in Publisher:

1 Select File, Page Setup, and choose landscape.

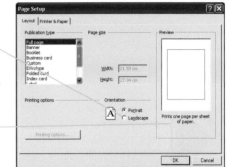

2 The paper dimensions are shown, with a preview pane and layout notes.

Layout guides, the blue and pink lines, are set initially to define the working area and the page margins. The CLAiT exercise requires specific margin sizes, which may be different from the default.

To view the current settings and if necessary set new layout guides:

1 Select from the Menu bar, Arrange, Layout Guides.

2 Use the arrows or type in the boxes to adjust the positions of the Margin guides as required.

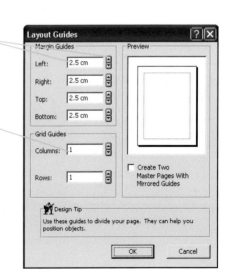

3 Specifying the number of columns in the Margin guides may be helpful, especially if you use Connected Text Boxes for multicolumn text (see page 133).

Templates

In this initial template only the margin guides have been set. You can create templates that have complex layouts with gridlines, logos and other items included.

Having created the required page layout, with margin guides, you can save it as a Template. Creating a template means that this layout can be used repeatedly, you just need to select which template to use when you start. To save as a Template:

1 Select File, Save As. Click on the down arrow on the Save as type box and change the file type to a Publisher Template.

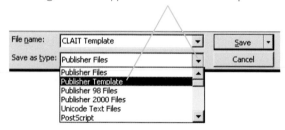

If you continue to work when you have saved your template, you must use Save As to rename the exercise and save it as a regular Publisher file or it will overwrite your template.

2 The Save in folder changes automatically to the Templates folder. You may see other Templates listed. Type in the file name and click on Save. Note that the template keeps the .pub file extension, the same as the normal file extension for Publisher documents.

To use a saved or existing Template:

Note, it's easiest to use the Task Pane to access the Templates. They are saved into a subfolder deep in the folder system, and are not easily found.

3 Select File, New. This opens the Publisher Task Pane and Publication Gallery (see page 127). At the foot of the task pane, select New, From Template.

To access Templates in previous versions of Publisher, click the Templates button at the bottom of the Wizard panel.

4 This opens the Templates folder, and displays the available templates. Select the template name and click Create New. This creates a new publication, not a new template.

Frames and boxes

Many of the Publisher tools deal with Frames which are containers for images, clip art and tables. Text is created or imported into a Text Box, also known as a Text Frame (the term used in previous versions of Publisher). DTP is in essence the management, manipulation and layout of these frames and boxes.

To create a Text Box:

1 Select the Text Box tool, by clicking on it and letting go. Move the mouse to the page area and the arrow becomes a large + (plus), also known as Cross-hairs.

2 Position the centre of the cross-hairs on the outer margin guide. Hold down the left mouse button, and drag down and across diagonally.

3 Release the mouse button, and Selection Handles appear at the corners and on the sides of the box. There are similar Selection Handles for an active picture frame.

Text box

4 To resize, position the mouse over a selection handle and you will get an arrow indicating the direction in which you will resize:

Horizontally RESIZE   Vertically RESIZE   Diagonally RESIZE

If you don't get the moving van symbol, just the cross, select Tools, Options, User Assistance, and tick Use helpful mouse pointers.

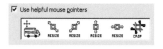

5   To move a frame, position the mouse pointer on the edge of the frame. It will change to the four-headed cross symbol, with a moving van. Just press the left mouse button and drag to the required location.

6   To delete a text box, press Shift+Delete. Pressing just Delete will delete the selected text within the box. To delete a picture frame, select the frame and press the Delete key.

It's easy to create text boxes by accident when you first start using Publisher. Any little grey boxes should be selected and deleted. See page 142 for information on the Design Checker which will check for empty frames.

Text box layout

For the heading text box you will need to create a separate frame, which will be up to the full page width, within the specified margins and its depth will be dependant on the size and style of font you choose.

The body text, which is the imported text file, will occupy much of the page and must be laid out in two or more columns as in a newsletter. To create a column layout in one text box:

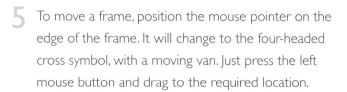

1   Click in the main or body text box. Select Format Text Box from the menu, click the Text Box tab, and press the Columns button.

2   Choose the number of columns. The Preview panel shows you the results of your choice. Columns created this way are sure to be equal in width.

Using this method the column widths remain equal, even if you change the size of the frame. You can also set the column gutter (space between the text) very easily.

3   The Spacing box allows you to specify the column gutter or space between the text in adjacent columns. The amount selected is shared between the adjacent columns.

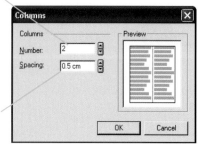

Connected frames

As an alternative to creating one text box with two or more columns, create a number of text boxes and connect them.

If you don't see the Connect Frames toolbar, select Views, Toolbars and click Connect Frames.

1 Create a series of text boxes on the page. For New CLAiT they must be the same width so you can use the column guide to help, or you can copy and paste the first frame, which is much easier.

You must keep your column widths equal. If you need to resize one frame to accommodate text, you must resize the others.

2 Select the first frame, so the selection handles appear. Click on the Create Text Box Link button on the Connect Frames toolbar.

3 The mouse pointer becomes a pitcher or jug, and will tip when you move it into the second text box. Click to complete the connection. The frames are now linked, and when you import text it will flow from one frame to the next.

If you forget to connect the frames together before you import the text file, and the text will overfill the current frame, Publisher will offer to connect the frames for you. See page 135 for Text in overflow.

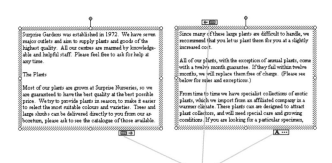

Surprise Gardens was established in 1972. We have seven major outlets and aim to supply plants and goods of the highest quality. All our centres are manned by knowledge-able and helpful staff. Please feel free to ask for help at any time.

The Plants

Most of our plants are grown at Surprise Nurseries, so we are guaranteed to have the best quality at the best possible price. We try to provide plants in season, to make it easier to select the most suitable colours and varieties. Trees and large shrubs can be delivered directly to you from our ar-boretum, please ask to see the catalogue of those available.

Since many of these large plants are difficult to handle, we recommend that you let us plant them for you at a slightly increased cost.

All of our plants, with the exception of annual plants, come with a twelve month guarantee. If they fail within twelve months, we will replace them free of charge. (Please see below for rules and exceptions.)

From time to time we have specialist collections of exotic plants, which we import from an affiliated company in a warmer climate. These plants can be designed to attract plant collectors, and will need special care and growing conditions. If you are looking for a particular specimen,

You must also ensure that the column gutter is correct, as no tolerance is allowed. Remember that Publisher allows 1 mm between the text and each frame so include this in your calculations.

5.500, 8.500 cm.   4.000 x 4.500 cm.

4 You'll see a link indicator at the bottom of the first text box. Click on the link to move to the next text box. The last text box has a link indicator at the top, connecting back to the previous box. If the text overflows the combined boxes, there's an indicator at the bottom showing Text in Overflow.

5 To set the size and spacing of frames you will need to use the Object Position and Object Size indicators on the Status bar.

Import text

You can type text into a text box, or you can use text created in another application and import it. In the CLAiT exercise you will usually type the heading into the heading frame, but import the text into the main text box. This is because the emphasis is on the placement and management of the text.

To import the text:

1 Create a text box and make sure it is the active frame. Select Insert, Text File. If an image frame, or no frame is selected, the Text File option will be greyed (unavailable).

2 The Insert Text dialog box opens My Documents folder. Navigate the folders if necessary to find the text file.

It shows files of all text formats, including Publisher and Word.

3 When you have found the file, select it and click OK.

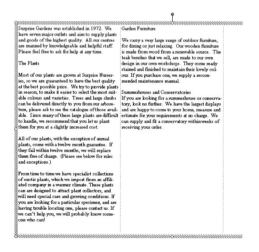

4 The text will be inserted into the frame, and will flow into the columns.

5 Note that if your text box is not large enough, you will get a warning message. See page 135.

Overflow text

When you import text you may not be sure how big the text box needs to be. The amount of text and the font size are the critical factors.

1 If the text box is too small, you will be warned that the inserted text doesn't fit the frame and offered the option of linking existing text boxes, or of creating new text boxes to

Frames and boxes in Publisher can be easily resized, you don't need to get the size right the first time.

hold the text. Click No to retain control of the process. The text will be placed into the box, flow through the columns if specified, and the Text in Overflow indicator will appear at the bottom.

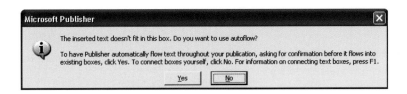

2 If you have created two or more linked text boxes, Publisher will connect the frames and flow the text through them. However, if they are still not big enough, Publisher will offer to create another frame. Again, select No and the Text in Overflow indicator will appear, below the last text box.

Once you have all the text showing, it's a good idea to make a note of the last few words of the text, just to make sure that they are showing when you print.

3 All you have to do is keep stretching the text box or frames, resizing until the frame is big enough and the symbol disappears.

To keep the text box the same size, click in the box, select Format Text Box, Text Box and choose Best Fit. The font size will be adjusted so that the text just fits.

4 The Text in Overflow symbol may appear when you resize the body text font, or when you move and resize images.

5 It may also appear when you enter text in a large font size into the heading frame. Again, just stretch the frame, or shrink the text.

Fonts

Font styles

For the New CLAiT course, you are required to use two different font styles, serif and sans serif fonts.

These terms, serif and sans serif, refer to the style of font. There are over a hundred fonts available in Publisher, with varying names, that match these styles. When you are doing any of the exercises, its fun to experiment. When you do the exam it's a good idea to stick to the recommended standard.

1. Serif fonts are those fonts where the letters have a stroke across the bottom of the letter. The standard serif font is Times New Roman.

Times New Roman Serif Font

2. Sans serif fonts are those where there is no line at the base. The standard suggested font is Arial.

Arial Sans Serif Font

3. To use a particular font, create the text box and select the style before you type. Alternatively, type the text in the default font, select the text and then apply the required font style.

4. Publisher will list the styles in the Font Schemes task pane. The fonts are named using their own type faces and they are displayed in groups that look good together.

Font Sizes

The amount of text, image size and choice of heading size will affect each other and it may vary from exercise to exercise, so be prepared to be flexible.

You will be required to display three differing sizes of text – a main heading size, a subheading size and a body text size. If the exact font size is not given, choose from these ranges:

Body text	–	10 to 14 point
Subheading	–	16 to 18 point
Main heading	–	24 to 28 point

Text alignment

You need to be working in a text box for the alignment buttons to be available.

The required text alignment will vary from frame to frame. The heading text, which you type in, will need to be centred across columns and to reach almost to each margin. The body text alignment will be changed during the exercise to demonstrate control. The alignment buttons are the same as used in Word. See page 40 for more details. To apply the alignment:

1 Click in each paragraph and select the required alignment. It will be applied to the whole paragraph.

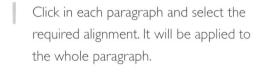

Remember to use the zoom feature when you are working with text. Zoom in to select the text, and zoom out to check the alignment.

2 Alternatively, press Ctrl+A to select everything within the text box, and then select the alignment. Be careful if the alignment for the subheadings should be different.

You will be required to indent part of the text. This means moving the first line or a whole paragraph, whichever is specified, to the right. To indent text:

3 Position the cursor in the paragraph that you need to indent. Select Format, Indents and Lists.

You can use the Format Painter to apply the first line indent to the second and subsequent paragraphs. See the Hot Tip on page 39 for more details.

4 For a first line indent click on the up arrow to the required amount, or type the value into the box. You will see a preview in the Sample pane. You can also use this dialog box to set paragraph alignment and line spacing.

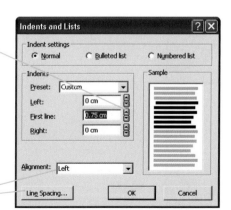

If you use Ctrl+A and select everything in the frame, your subheadings will be treated as a first line and will also be indented.

Import an image file

Use Publisher's Help facility to see all the picture file formats you can import into Publisher. Search for "graphics file formats and filters".

Publisher allows you to insert both Clip Art images and images from other sources into your publication. It provides two separate buttons and menu entries: the Clip Art option opens the Clip Organizer, and the Picture from File opens the My Pictures folder. To import a picture file:

 Picture frame

 Clip Organizer Frame

To insert a Clip Art image, select the Clip Organizer Frame button to display the Insert Clip Art task pane, and search for an image. When you Insert the image, a clip art frame is created automatically.

1   Select the Picture Frame button. Move the mouse pointer to the page area where it becomes crosshairs. Position the mouse where you want the image, hold down the left mouse button and draw a box frame (initially square).

2   Choose Insert, Picture, From File. My Pictures folder will open. You may need to browse the folders to find the image file.

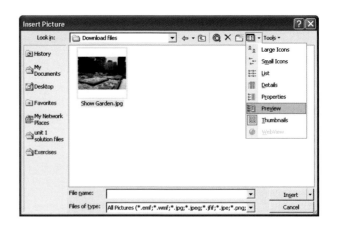

To help in selecting the correct image, use the Preview facility.

The image can be adjusted if it is the wrong size or in the wrong location. See page 139.

3   Click on Insert and the image will be inserted into the frame. The image will be resized to fit the frame width. The frame height will be adjusted to keep the correct proportions. Note that if you had just clicked the page, instead of drawing a frame, the image will be inserted full size.

Image management

When you first start the CLAiT exercise, read it through and take particular notice of how you will need to change the image. If you are asked to make it bigger, start with a small image, and vice versa.

To resize an image:

1 Use the white selection handle on any corner, not on the sides. Dragging the corner handles maintains the image proportions.

The frame automatically adjusts to the correct ratio when you insert the image the first time, whatever shape frame you created.

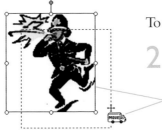

To move an image:

2 Position the mouse pointer on any edge, avoiding the selection handles. When it changes to the Moving van symbol, drag to the required position.

To rotate an image:

3 Hold the mouse over the green Rotation handle until it changes, then click and drag to the required angle. Press Shift to rotate 15 degrees at a time.

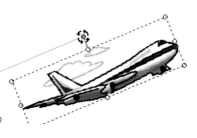

Select the wrapping style that meets the requirements of the exercise. Usually this will be Square, or Top and bottom:

When you have column text, make sure that the image is no more than the width of a column.

To flip an image:

4 Select the image and from the Menu click Arrange, Rotate or Flip and then, usually, Flip Horizontal.

To fit an image to text:

5 When you place an image in a Text Box, you will need to select Format Picture from the Picture toolbar and choose the Layout tab. Click the Wrapping Style you'd like to use.

Drawing tools

You can use the Line Tool to draw a line under the heading, or between two columns of text. You can use the Rectangle Tool to draw a box around the heading or image. You can also use the Frame Border option, see page 141.

To use the drawing tools, select the tool and move to the page area. Position the crosshairs where you wish to begin, and just drag to draw the shape. Shapes can be resized and moved just like images and text boxes.

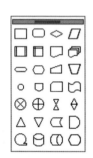

1 The Line Tool draws a line between any two points. To keep to a strict horizontal, vertical or 45 degree angle, hold down the Shift key as you drag.

2 The Arrow tool also draws a line, but adds an arrow head at one end or both ends.

3 The Oval Tool draws an oval, and makes it a true circle if you hold down the Shift key whilst dragging.

4 The Rectangle Tool draws a box, which will be an exact square if you hold down Shift as you drag.

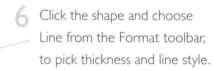

The contents of the Formatting and Picture toolbars change, depending on which type of object has been selected.

5 Click on AutoShapes to draw stars, banners, U-turns and many other shapes, just like AutoShapes in PowerPoint (see page 157).

6 Click the shape and choose Line from the Format toolbar, to pick thickness and line style.

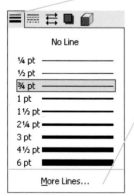

No Line
¼ pt
½ pt
¾ pt
1 pt
1½ pt
2¼ pt
3 pt
4½ pt
6 pt
More Lines…

7 Click on More Lines to see the complete range of options, to change the colour or to select a dashed line style. Click OK to apply the changes.

Borders

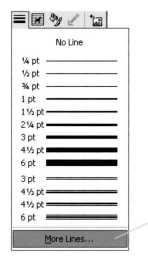

To put a border around a text or image frame:

1. Select the Line/Border Style button from the Picture toolbar, and pick  a line style and width. Notice that the selection offered is greater than for AutoShapes (see page 140).

2. For more choice and greater control, select More Lines (or click Format Picture on the Picture toolbar).

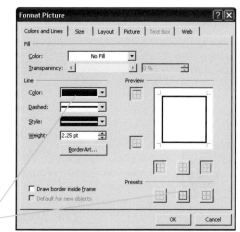

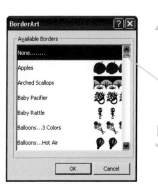

You will find more border styles in the Clip Art Organizer.

3. To put a border around the whole object select Box and then the colour and thickness. You will see the effect in the Preview panel.

4. For a special effect, click the Border Art button, and select a picture that will be replicated as a border on all four sides of the selected object.

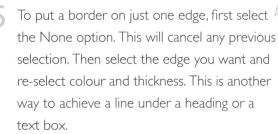

5. To put a border on just one edge, first select the None option. This will cancel any previous selection. Then select the edge you want and re-select colour and thickness. This is another way to achieve a line under a heading or a text box.

Final publication layout

The finished publication must always meet the requirements of the CLAiT exercise.

A degree of variation between presentations is expected as image sizes and choice of heading and subheading font sizes can affect the publication layout. The final step is to balance the columns so that each column finishes at about the same point on the page. Publisher has a Line Spacing facility that allows you to fine tune the spacing, making it easier to achieve a balanced page.

Three sizes of font, heading, subheading and body text, must be obviously discernible. Your choice of Serif and Sans Serif fonts must clearly display the difference in style.

1 Press Ctrl+A to select all the text, then click Format, Line Spacing.

Make sure that the text does not overflow the text box when you change the paragraph spacing.

2 You will need to experiment with the various spacings to achieve the balanced columns and full page layout requirement. A tolerance of two lines difference in column length is accepted.

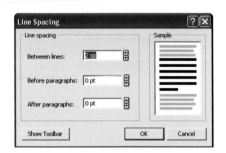

The Design Checker

Publisher provides the Design Checker to examine your finished document for potential problems and help with resolving them. You may, for example, have created empty text boxes, or have text hidden in an overflow area.

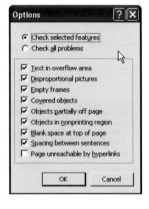

The Design Checker does not check your margins for you.

1 Select Tools, Design Checker, and the options button. Tick the items to check and click OK.

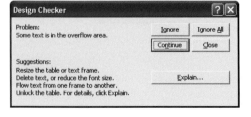

You can work with the document to correct problems whilst this dialog box is still open.

2 When you run the Design Checker, it identifies problems and offers solutions and explanations.

Printing publications

You are required for the New CLAiT course to print a composite publication. Put simply, it just means producing a print that shows all the elements of the finished item. Professional printing companies would require a composite and a series of colour separation prints. These show the breakdown of individual colours onto separate printing plates. Publisher has Commercial Printing Tools that allow you to print to commercial specifications.

1 Select Tools, Commercial Printing Tools, Colour Printing to see the options.

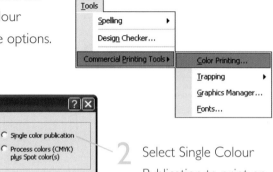

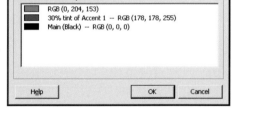

2 Select Single Colour Publication to print on a monochrome printer, and print in black and greyscales.

3 Using the normal File, Print, will produce the composite print, which is the format required for CLAiT exercises.

4 To print the text part of the publication for proofreading, select File, Print, and click the Advanced Print Settings button. Choose Do not print any graphics and it will put placeholders on the page.

Unit 4 exercise

You are allowed two and a half hours to complete this exercise.

Scenario

You are working as an assistant at Surprise Garden Centres. You are required to create a two-fold, three section advertising flyer for the company. To complete this exercise you will need the files Surprise Garden Centres.txt and Show Garden.jpg.

Task 1

Before you begin the exercise, make a subfolder called Unit 4 in the CLAiT Coursework folder as a storage area to contain your answers.

1. Create a new single-page publication.
2. Set up as a master page or template the following:

Page size	A4
Page orientation	landscape
Top/bottom margins	3 cms
Left/right margins	2.5 cms

3. Create a text box in the top margin and add your name.
4. Set up the page layout in a newsletter format, to include a page wide heading above three columns of text.

column widths	equal
space between columns	0.75 cm

5. Enter the heading SURPRISE OUTDOOR LIVING CENTRES at the top of the page using a sans serif font.
6. Increase the size of the heading text so that it extends across the full width of all the columns of text. There should be no more than 2 cms of blank space between the heading and the left and right margins. Make sure that the heading text is centred on the page.
7. Import the text file Surprise Garden Centres so that it begins at the top of the left hand column, below the heading. The text should flow through the columns.
8. Create a text box in the footer area and type the file name Flyer 1.
9. Save the file as Flyer 1.
10. Print a composite copy of the document.

You'll also find the image file in the Unit 4 folder, within the NC2006data folder.

Task 2

Using the same file, Flyer1:

1. Format the body text to be left-aligned, in a serif font.
2. Spell check the document and correct the four spelling mistakes.
3. Import the image Show Garden.jpg, and place it in the centre of the left-hand column. Make the image large enough to almost fill the width of the column, whilst maintaining the image proportions. Make sure that it does not cover any text.

4. Edit the filename in the footer text to Flyer 2.
5. Save the file with the file name Flyer 2.
6. Print one composite copy of the publication for your manager. Make sure that the printed publication fits onto one page.
7. Check your document to ensure that you have completed all the requirements.

Task 3

You have been asked to make the following amendments:

1. Make the image smaller, keeping the proportions, and move it into the middle of the central column.
2. Arrange the image so that the column text is above and below only. Make sure that the image does not extend into the columns on either side.

3.   Flip the image horizontally.

4.   Increase the size of the subheadings, The Plants, Garden Furniture and Summerhouses and Conservatories, so that they are larger than the body text, but smaller than the page heading.

5.   Change the body text to be fully justified, in a serif font.

6.   Edit the filename in the footer text to Flyer 3.

7.   Save the file as Flyer 3.

8.   Print one composite copy of the publication.

Task 4

1.   Change the subheading Summerhouses and Conservatories to Conservatories and Garden Rooms.

To help with balancing columns, you can change the image size, the font sizes and the line spacing.

2.   Draw a single vertical line between each of the columns of text. The line weight should be 2¼ pt. The lines should not overlap or obscure any text or extend into the margin area.

3.   Format the body text so that the first line of each paragraph is indented by 0.5 cms. Make sure that the subheadings are not indented.

4.   Increase the size of the body text so that the columns are balanced at the bottom of the page. Make sure that the headings, subheadings and body text are still different sizes.

5.   Edit the footer text to Flyer 4.

6.   Save the file as Flyer 4 and print a composite copy. Your printed publication should fit on one page.

At the end of this exercise you should have four prints:

Flyer 1

Flyer 2

Flyer 3

Flyer 4

Create an e-Presentation

In this unit we use PowerPoint to develop an understanding of graphical presentation concepts. It covers creating a master layout, importing an image and applying standard formatting to create a consistent and professional presentation.

Covers

Presentation graphics | 148

Slide layouts | 149

The Slide Master | 150

Slide Master text | 152

Insert an image | 153

Applying a slide layout | 154

Bulleted text | 155

Text tools | 156

Autoshapes | 157

Arranging slides | 158

Printing | 159

The Slide Show | 161

Unit 5 exercise | 162

Unit Five

Presentation graphics

PowerPoint is the presentation graphics program included with Microsoft Office. With it you can design, create and organise presentations in many formats, from handouts and transparencies, to sophisticated and automated shows run on the computer.

From the Taskbar, click Start, All Programs, Microsoft PowerPoint.

1 The program opens with the default blank presentation. The first view shows the Title slide in landscape layout, ready to begin a new presentation. The two text boxes are used as placeholders.

The term Slide refers to each page in a PowerPoint presentation, whether it is printed on paper, as a transparency, or just viewed in a screen show.

The Task Pane is a very useful addition to the PowerPoint window. Click View, Task Pane if it does not appear automatically.

PowerPoint provides an area for you to add speaker notes for each slide. These will not be displayed.

2 On the right, the Task Pane lists possible actions. PowerPoint, in common with many other Office programs, provides design templates and a Wizard to help with layout, colour and content.

3 The pane to the left of the window allows you to switch between Outline and Slides view and provides an overview as you build the presentation.

Slide layouts

PowerPoint provides standard slide layouts, or templates, that you can use to present your information.

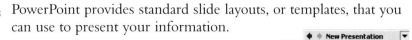

1 Click the down arrow on the New Presentation Task pane, and select Slide Layout to view the available layout templates.

2 Hover the mouse over each slide to see its name and style. The first block of four slides are for text only. The Title slide is displayed when you open PowerPoint.

3 The Title Only and Title and Text slides provide the layouts needed for the CLAiT exercises.

4 Content Layouts show a number of configurations. They include designs with placeholders for tables, charts, Clip Art and WordArt. Scroll down to see other examples including Organisation charts. There is also a blank layout.

5 When you insert a new slide, select it from this Task pane. Click the arrow on the selected slide layout and choose Insert New Slide.

6 Note the checked box to show these designs when inserting new slides.

The Slide Master

To create a professional looking presentation, you should implement a house style using a standard layout and consistent formatting. PowerPoint provides the Slide Master to enable you to do this. You can insert an image or background on the Slide Master, position text boxes, format text styles and add standard text. That configuration will be applied to all the slides in the presentation.

To create a Slide Master:

1 Select View, Master, Slide Master.

2 The Slide Master provides placeholders for a title, text content, and standard autotext areas for date/time, footer, and slide number. The text boxes can be resized and moved if required.

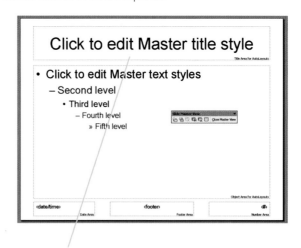

3 Click in the Title Area and use the Formatting toolbar to select the font size, style, alignment and attributes such as bold or italic that you wish to apply.

See page 155 for how to manage indentation and the hierarchical levels.

4 The main text box displays bulleted and indented text. Each level is represented by a different bullet style, size of font and degree of indentation. Select each level in turn and if necessary adjust the font size and any attributes.

Text boxes are provided on most slide layouts. You can also create your own text boxes if needed, and position them where required. Select Insert, Text Box from the menu. See page 131 for more details on creating and working with text boxes.

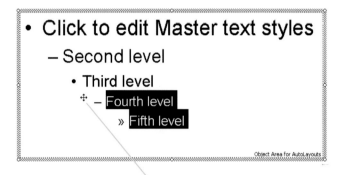

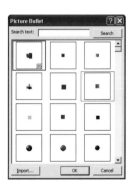

5 The Slide Master shows a hierarchy of five levels of bullets. The four-headed arrow that appears when the mouse is to the left of the text, allows you to select several levels and work with them as a group.

6 To change the bullet symbol, select Format, Bullets and Numbering and choose from the styles available. Click Customise to select a new style from a vast range of fonts. Click Picture to add even more stylish and coloured bullets. To remove Bullets, select None. You can apply and remove Bullets using the toolbar button which is a toggle switch.

The Numbering function works in the same way as the Bullets.

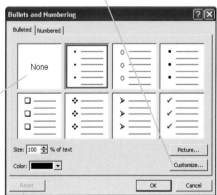

Slide Master text

The Slide Master is for design, colour, text and images that you want to show on every slide. Add the Title and other text in Normal view.

For text to appear on every slide in the same place, same font etc, you need to put it on the Slide Master. At the bottom of the Slide Master are three pre-defined text areas.

The Date Area and the Number Area can contain automatic fields, such as we saw in headers and footers in Word. These fields will be automatically updated when changes are made, for example changing the order of the slides. To activate these fields and have footer text appear on all slides:

Creating, editing, deleting and spell checking text is the same in PowerPoint as it is in Word. See pages 31-33.

1 Open the Slide Master and click on View, on the Menu bar and then Header and Footer.

2 Tick the box to Include on slide Date and time. Select to Update automatically and click the down arrow next to the date to select the date format. You must ensure that you select an English date format and you may be required to display the time as well.

Selecting a Fixed date means you can type in the date to display. You would have to change this date manually if you wanted to update it.

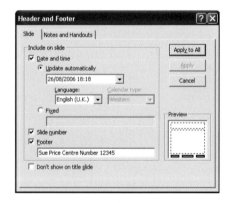

The Apply to all button is the only option, as you are working with the Master slide.

3 Also tick the box for Slide number. Finally tick the Footer option and type any required text. In the Preview pane, on the right, you will see that all three boxes in the footer area are black (active).

Insert an image

With the Slide Master displayed, select Insert, Picture, From File. The default folder that opens is My Pictures. You may need to navigate the folders to locate the image.

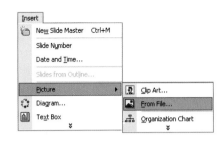

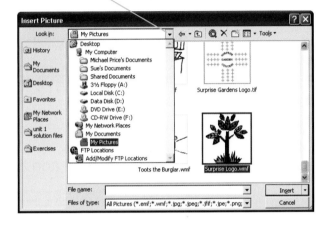

2 Click Insert and the selected graphic will be inserted centrally with its selection handles displayed. Drag it to the required position using the arrowhead mouse symbol.

3 To ensure that the text and image frames do not conflict, you may need to resize the main text frame. Position the mouse on the selection handle and drag.

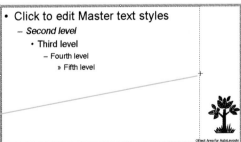

Applying a slide layout

When you have created the Slide Master, save the file using the standard Office procedure and the supplied filename.

The completed Slide Master will provide the template for the slides you create in this presentation.

1 Select View, Normal to return to the standard slide view, or click on the Normal View icon at the bottom of the screen.

2 The text and image that were inserted onto the Slide Master are displayed and the standard Title slide layout applied.

For every Slide Master, you can create a Title Master. The Title Master adheres to the formatting applied to the Slide Master, but not the layout. You may need to amend the Title Master if there is a subtitle that causes a conflict between text and graphic.

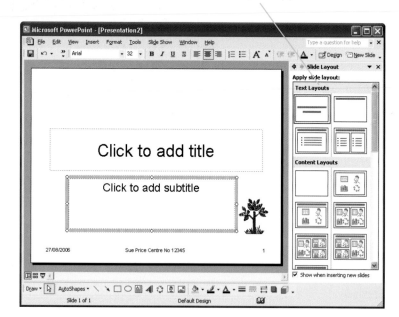

You can select and delete any unwanted text boxes, such as the subtitle frame.

3 If you require a different layout, click the style you want to use. Alternatively you can click the arrow to access the shortcut options. The new layout is applied, affecting any existing slide or slides which are currently selected.

4 Add your text in the placeholders. When you click in the text area the existing text will disappear.

Bulleted text

The Slide Master showed the bullet levels and allowed you to specify the formats. See page 151.

PowerPoint provides five levels of bulleted text. Each bullet point is ascribed a level of importance, illustrated by the font size and degree of indentation. When the bullet point is promoted or demoted, both the bullet symbol and the text format are adjusted.

1 Select a layout that contains bulleted text. The bullets appear automatically on the first line and as you press Enter.

2 To apply a lower level bullet, or demote text, press Tab once for each level, before you begin to type. Use Shift+Tab to promote text.

The Increase and Decrease Indent buttons can also be used to promote and demote bulleted text.

3 You can drag a bullet to promote or demote. The text will move one level at a time. Any lower level points will also be adjusted.

 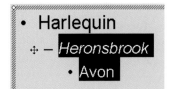

For consistency on your slides, any changes to the bullet layout should be made on the Master slide.

4 Bullet spacing and indentation is controlled through the Ruler, available on the View menu.

5 Drag the top triangle marker to move the bullet point, or the lower triangle marker to move the text. To move both and keep the existing spacing relationship, drag the rectangle on the bottom marker. You cannot promote or demote bullets this way.

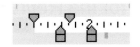

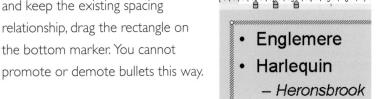

Text tools

For New CLAiT purposes Autofit Text may cause problems if a specific text size is required.

Autofit Text

PowerPoint provides an Autofit Text option that may adjust the text size to fit the placeholder. A Smart Tag appears when the amount of text will overfill the frame. You will need to evaluate each situation individually to see the effect. In some instances the line spacing is slightly adjusted, in others the text is resized. Click on control AutoCorrect options to make changes to the AutoFit setup.

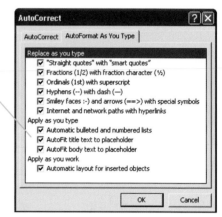

From the Menu select Tools, Options and the Spelling and Style tab.

The Spell Checker

Automatic spell checking should be enabled when you start PowerPoint. Any misspelled words will be underlined in red. Note that the default option is to ignore words in uppercase and words with numbers, so proof reading is essential. Click the Style Options button to see the underlying concepts of standard design, such as upper and lowercase conventions and number of bullet points per slide.

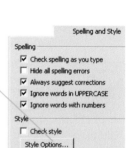

PowerPoint offers a subset of the Word Find and Replace facility, as slides generally contain minimal text. You will need to check capitalisation of the replacing word (all capitals, lower or sentence case) as PowerPoint does not honour existing case.

Find and Replace

From the Menu select Edit, Find. Type in the 'Find What' text and click the Replace button to display the Replace With box. Replace works forwards from the cursor, Replace All covers the whole document and will inform you of the number replaced.

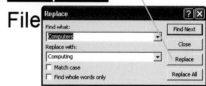

Autoshapes

Using Autoshapes adds another dimension to a presentation. PowerPoint provides a multitude of shapes that can be created, resized and placed on the slide with a minimum of effort. To view and use Autoshapes:

Stars and Banners

Callouts

1 Select Insert, Picture, Autoshapes.

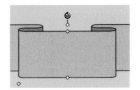

2 Hover the mouse over each of the icons on the Autoshape toolbar to view the description of its content. There are eight basic categories, including lines, arrows, flowchart symbols, stars and banners and callouts.

Use the green rotation point to change the angle of the shape.

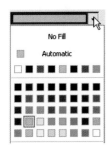

3 Click on the required shape and move the crosshair mouse symbol to the slide area.

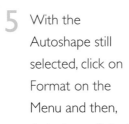

4 Press the left mouse button and draw the shape. It will automatically expand as you move the mouse. Use the corner selection handles to resize, and the four headed arrow to move the shape.

5 With the Autoshape still selected, click on Format on the Menu and then, Autoshape. Select a Fill colour for the shape and click OK.

Arranging slides

The standard PowerPoint window displays an extra pane with Outline and Slides views. The Outline view shows the slide text, so you can see the development of your document. The Slides view gives the impression of layout, spacing and overall presentation. Either view will enable you to change the order of the slides. However, if you have lots of slides use Slide Sorter View.

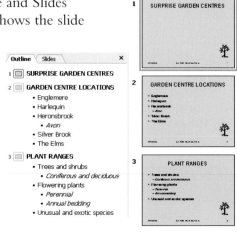

To change the magnification of either of these panes, click on the pane and use the standard zoom option.

100% ▼
100%
75%
66%
50%
33%
25%

Change the width of the pane using the double headed arrow that appears on the dividing bar.

1 Select View, Slide Sorter.

View	
▣	Normal
▦	Slide Sorter
	Zoom…

2 Click on the slide you wish to reposition and drag it to its new location. You will see the Move symbol attached to the mouse, and a large vertical line indicating its new position.

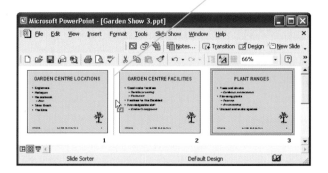

If you wish to start and end with the same slide, Slide Sorter view allows copy and paste of slides.

3 Slide Sorter view is used to set up an automated show. Transition effects, such as checkerboards and blinds, can be applied and the show previewed. See page 161 for more details on slide shows.

Printing

You will usually be expected to print the slides, one per page, and thumbnail or handouts at a specified number per page.

1 Select File, Page Setup. The slides are sized for an On-screen show, but you may wish to select a paper size.

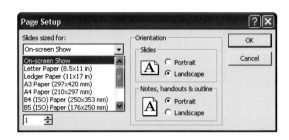

2 Select File, Print, to access the printing options. Select All slides, or a range of slides to print.

It's a good idea to proof read the finished prints. Errors are much more easily spotted on paper.

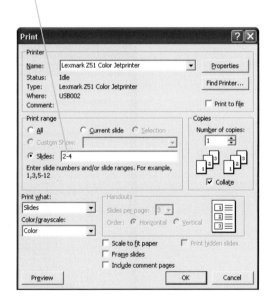

3 Slides are the default choice, and will be printed one slide per page in landscape orientation.

4 To print reduced size slides, or Thumbnails, select Handouts from the Print What box.

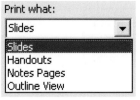

...cont'd

PowerPoint makes it easy to share presentations, offering Send to Mail Recipients (for Review) or (as Attachment). It also provides a Pack and Go wizard to enable you to transfer the presentation to another computer.

5 Select the number per page, from one to nine. Handouts will include lines for audience notes at the side if you select three per page. Check the Preview panel for the slide layout.

6 Select Outline View from the Print What box for a more compact and text only view of the presentation.

You can re-select the print format from the menu bar in the Print Preview window.

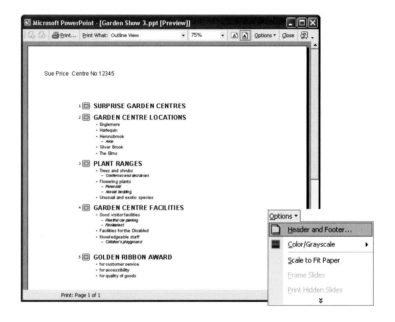

When you print the individual slides, one per page, they will already have a header or footer with your name and Centre number.

7 Click Print Preview, or Preview on the main Print dialog box to confirm that you are printing the required layout.

8 Click Options on the Preview menu to apply a Header or Footer to the Handouts, Notes or Outline View prints.

The Slide Show

The Slide Show is a major feature of PowerPoint. It is not required for the New CLAiT 2006 course, but it's quite easy to create and very effective.

1 Select Slide Sorter view, and pick the Slide Transition Task pane.

2 Transition effects are applied as the slide appears on the monitor. Select a slide and choose a Transition effect.

3 Some effects can be quite dramatic, so it is best to stay with the same one or two throughout the show.

4 The speed can be adjusted, and sound applied. For fully automated shows, you can choose to advance to the next slide automatically after a set time.

5 Click the Slide Show button to go straight to the show. Click the mouse to proceed from slide to slide. The show will end with a black screen. Click the mouse, or press Escape to return to the PowerPoint editing view.

The standard file extension for PowerPoint is .ppt. Save the presentation as a .pps file to have it run automatically on start up.

6 The slide text can be animated. Switch to Normal view and select the Slide Design – Animation Scheme Task pane. Click the Play button to see the effect. In this example, text is appearing from the bottom right.

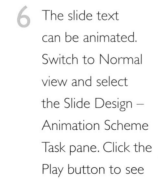

Unit 5 exercise

You are allowed two and a half hours to complete this exercise.

You'll find the Surprise Logo image in the Unit 5 folder, within the NC2006data folder downloaded from the In Easy Steps web site (see page 253).

Scenario

You are working as an assistant for Surprise Gardens. You have been asked to provide a slide show presentation for the headquarters foyer. To complete this exercise you will need the file Surprise Logo.wmf.

You have to produce a presentation of four slides.

Task 1

1. Create a master slide as follows:

    Create a page-wide title frame at the top of the page.

    Create a page-wide main frame below the title frame.

    Set up the text styles in these frames as follows:

Frame	Style	Emphasis	Size	Alignment
Title	Title	Bold	40-44	Centre
Main	1st level bullet	None	28-32	Left
Main	2nd level bullet	Italic	20-24	Left and indented

Surprise Logo.wmf

2. Import the image Surprise Logo.wmf and place it at the bottom right corner of the slide. Make sure it does not overlap or obscure any text frames.

3. Add your name, exam centre number, an automatic date and the slide number to the footer area of the slide.

4. Save the master slide using the filename Garden Show. This master slide is to be used for all four slides.

Before you begin the exercise, you could make a subfolder called Unit 5 in the CLAiT Coursework folder as a storage area to contain your presentation.

Task 2

1. Create slide 1 and enter the title SURPRISE GARDEN CENTRES.

2. Create slide 2 and enter the title:
    GARDEN CENTRE LOCATIONS

3. Enter the following text in the main frame, using the styles shown:

Englemere	1st level
Harlequin	1st level

Heronsbrook	1st level
Avon	2nd level
Silver Brook	1st level
Rookery	2nd level
The Elms	1st level

4. Create slide 3 and enter the title:

   GARDEN CENTRE AMENITIES

5. Enter the following text in the main frame with the styles shown:

Good visitor amenities	1st level
Plentiful car parking	2nd level
Amenities for the Disabled	2nd level
Knowledgeable staff	1st level
Children's playground	1st level

6. Create slide 4 and enter the title:

   PLANT RANGES

7. Enter the following text in the main text frame with the styles shown:

Trees and shrubs	1st level
Coniferous and deciduous	2nd level
Flowering plants	1st level
Perennial	2nd level
Annual bedding	2nd level
Unusual and exotic species	1st level

8. Save the slide show keeping the file name Garden Show.

9. Print out each of the 4 slides, one per page.

Task 3

You have been asked to make a few changes to the presentation.

1. On slide 2, delete the line Rookery

2. Add the following line to slide 3, after Plentiful car parking, and before Amenities for the Disabled:

Restaurant	2nd level

3. On slide 3, demote Children's playground.

4. On the same slide, promote Amenities for the Disabled.

5. Replace the word Amenities with the word Facilities wherever it appears in the presentation (three times in all).

6. Amend the master slide to display a pale green background. This must appear on all slides.

7. Save the amended slide show as Garden Show 2.

8. Print slides 2, 3 and 4 as Handouts with all three on one page.

Task 4

1. Create a further slide, slide 5. Into the Title box insert the text: GOLDEN RIBBON AWARD.

2. In the body text box type:

for customer service	1st level bullet
for accessibility	1st level bullet
for quality of goods	1st level bullet

3. Beneath the bullet text insert an autoshape of a ribbon.

4. Fill the ribbon with a gold colour.

5. Move slide 4 to become slide 3.

6. Save the file as Garden Show 3.

7. Print an outline view of the presentation to display the text on all five slides.

8. Include your name and Centre Number in the header area of this print.

9. Close the presentation.

When you have completed this exercise you should have the following prints:

Four individual slide prints

A single page handout print with slides 2,3 and 4

A single page outline print of all the slides with your name and centre number in the header area.

e-Image Creation

This unit shows how to use image editor software to produce and print images and drawings. It includes import, crop and resize for images, and text manipulation and formatting. A colour printer and digital camera images will be required to carry out the exercise tasks.

Covers

Computer art | 166

The software | 168

Using Paint Shop Pro | 170

Create the canvas | 171

Load and insert image | 172

Resize image | 173

Resize and Crop | 174

Vector layers | 175

Draw preset shape | 176

Enter text | 177

Edit artwork | 178

Transfer digital photographs | 180

Change image resolution | 182

Print image | 183

Unit 6 exercise | 185

Unit Six

Computer art

You do not have to be artistic, or good at drawing to attempt this unit.

In this unit you are going to create a piece of artwork, composing a series of separate items into a specified design. The layout of the artwork is supplied, as are the images that you will need. Sizes, shapes and colours are specified, and to achieve the finished item, you will handle two different types of graphics, bitmap and vector.

Bitmap images

Bitmap images, also known as raster images, are based on pixels. Each pixel is a tiny block, containing one colour. If you were to zoom in on a bitmap image, you would eventually begin to see the picture breakdown into blocks or become pixelated.

The images that you will import in the exercise will be in the form of bitmap images.

The advantage of pixel based images is that each pixel can take a different shade of colour, thus providing depth, shadow and texture to images. Bitmap images are used for photographs and most pictures you will see on the Internet.

The most common file formats used for bitmaps are:

There is a bewildering number of different graphics file formats used. Nearly every software program has its own 'native' file format. Always save your file in this native format before you save it in any other. You may for instance want to save it as a GIF or JPEG to send over the Internet.

- TIFF   Tag Image File Format
- JPEG   Joint Photographic Experts Group
- GIF   Graphical Interchange Format

The disadvantage of the bitmap format is that it does not resize well. If you resize a picture, making it larger, the software has to compensate and fill in the gaps. A dithering or antialiasing function is used to smooth out the differences in colour and lines. If you make the picture smaller, then it has to guess which pixels to drop, and so some of the detail gets lost.

Vector images

Vector graphics do not use pixels, instead they describe an image in terms of shapes, lines and text. They are based on mathematical formulae and measurements that represent lines and curves. Because they plot or draw a line between two points they are very smooth and have the great advantage that they can be scaled or resized. Vector graphics are particularly suited to geometric shapes, and will be used in this unit to draw lines and shapes.

Vector graphics use gradations of colour, but it is more difficult to create shading. They cannot represent irregular details and fine changes of texture or tint and are totally impossible for the level of detail found in photographs.

The most common vector file formats are:

Vectors are used for shapes and line drawings in the exercises, and they can also be used to define text, so that it can be easily resized.

- WMF   Windows Metafile
- AI   Adobe Illustrator
- EPS   Encapsulated Postscript

Resizing images

When an image is enlarged, the results depend on how the image was constructed. This can be demonstrated using a piece of text.

When you view an image on the screen, you see it at approximately 72 pixels to the inch. When you print it, your printer may achieve 300-600 dots per inch. The software has to fill in the extra dots, so what looks good on the screen, may not look quite so good when printed.

1   The first example is a scaled bitmap representation, which shows the stepped effect, that's found in pixelated images.

Abcde   **Abcde**

2   The second case shows the same text with antialiasing applied. Shades of grey help to smooth out the stepping.

Abcde   **Abcde**

3   With vectors however, text (or drawings) can be enlarged indefinitely without any loss of shape, as the final example illustrates.

Abcde   Abcde

The software

OCR does not make any recommendations or suggestions, but the education centre where you take your New CLAiT course may require that you use their specific choices.

You will require software that has vector drawing capabilities and image or photo editing capabilities. The required functions are spread across Microsoft Office products, such as Word, Publisher, PowerPoint and Visio. There are also tools such as Microsoft Office Photo Editor and Windows Paint or Picture and Fax Viewer. You'd need to use a combination of these to complete all the tasks in the exercises for this unit. Alternatively you could use a dedicated image editor such as those supplied by Corel or Adobe.

Corel software options

Corel provides the Paint Shop Pro image editing software. The products and versions supplied by Corel include:

You may have photo editing software supplied with your scanner or digital camera. You could use this to practise the exercises, but make sure that it can handle all the functions specified in the New CLAiT syllabus, since these applications are often Lite (lower function) versions.

- Paint Shop Pro Studio   (New or inexperienced users)
- Paint Shop Pro 9   (Intermediate and advanced users)
- Paint Shop Pro X   (Targets all levels of users)

For details of the software, go to the Corel web site at http://www.corel.co.uk, and select Products, Paint Shop Pro Family.

Paint Shop Pro is now owned by Corel Corporation, but was originally marketed by Jasc Software. If you have one of the older versions, for example PSP6, PSP7 or PSP8, these would serve equally well for the purposes of this unit.

2   Click the Try button to download a trial 30 day version.

Adobe software options

Adobe offers the Photoshop Creative Suite digital editing product. This is arguably the highest function solution available, and would satisfy professional graphics designer requirements.

Adobe Photoshop CS is part of the Adobe Creative Suite, which has, in addition to Photoshop, Illustrator, InDesign, GoLive and Acrobat products.

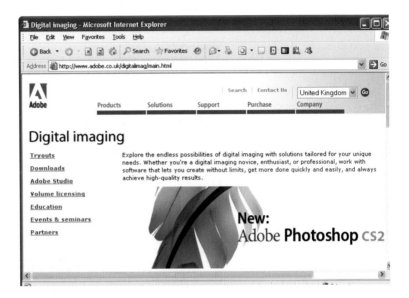

This is an expensive product for the more casual user, so Adobe also offers a lower cost alternative that still provides comprehensive image editing functions, in the form of the Photoshop Elements application.

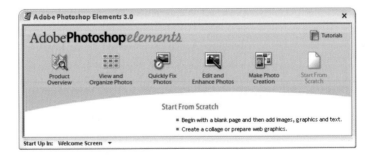

More details of these two products can be found at the Adobe web site http://www.adobe.com. Thirty day trial versions of either product may also be downloaded from that site.

Using Paint Shop Pro

The Studio edition of Paint Shop Pro (see page 168) *has been used to illustrate the steps in the exercises. However, you can follow similar steps with any image editors that offers suitable tools and functions.*

When you open Paint Shop Pro, it displays the work area, tool bars and palettes that you use to create, edit and print your art work images.

Menu bar   Standard toolbar   Title bar   Materials palette

Tool Options toolbar

Learning Center palette

Click the [X] button to hide the Learning Center palette and have more room for the image work area.

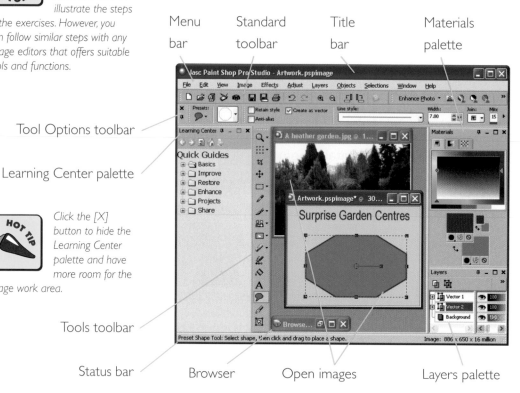

Tools toolbar

Status bar   Browser   Open images   Layers palette

When you save your file in the Paint Shop Pro .pspimage format, the layers are retained. When you reopen it you can still access individual layers. When you save the file as a .gif, .jpg or .tif, the layers will be merged, and vector images will be converted to raster.

The art work you are going to create starts with a canvas which sets the size of the finished work. The process of creating the art work requires you to work in layers, with the canvas being layer one. Each image that you use will be opened in a window, copied and pasted onto the art work as a separate layer. The individual file window can then be closed.

Similarly, when you add text or drawing shapes, they will be placed on a separate layer within the art work.

Working with layers in this way means that you can select a specific layer to make changes or adjustments to a particular section of the art work. You can also insert layers to create effects or to change factors such as the brightness or hue.

Create the canvas

Paint Shop Pro remembers anything that you specify. Next time you open this window it will have the details and dimensions that you set this time.

The canvas is your starting point. It lets you set both the size and resolution that will be used by the whole art work.

1 Paint Shop Pro opens with an empty grey screen. Select File, New or click the New button.

Choose an image resolution of 72 or 96 pixels per inch (ppi) for a canvas intended for web pages. An image resolution of 150 or 300 is typically selected for canvases that are ultimately meant to be printed.

2 Choose the measurement units first, (inches, centimetres or pixels) and then specify the size.

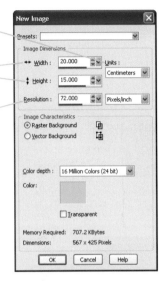

3 Select the canvas resolution, the number of pixels per inch or per centimetre.

The image resolution that is set on the original canvas is the resolution that will be used by all the images. The resolution, once set, controls the size of the finished product and should not be changed.

Once you have created the canvas, the size and the resolution are directly linked. If you change the image resolution, the physical dimensions will change as well.

If you have an image with a size of 10 cms by 8 cms and a resolution of 72 pixels per inch, when you place it on a canvas with a resolution of 150 pixels per inch, it effectively shrinks to approximately 5 cms by 4 cms. However, the number of pixels in the image will be unchanged.

The resolution also affects the memory required to work with the artwork. At 72 pixels/inch the memory required for the sample canvas is 700KBytes, at 150 it would be 1.6MBytes.

See page 182 for more illustrations of the effects of changing the resolution of the image.

4 Change the colour depth, if required. For example, choose 256 Colors if the art work is to become a GIF image.

2 Colors (1 bit)
16 Colors (4 bit)
Greyscale (8 bit)
256 Colors (8 bit)
16 Million Colors (24 bit)

5 Click the Color box to select the colour for the canvas. This becomes the background colour. See page 172 for an illustration.

Load and insert image

Select File, Browser, to use the Paint Shop Pro Studio Browser, to help you view, open, sort and manage your image files.

1 Select File, Open and locate the image that you need to add to the artwork. It will open in a new window.

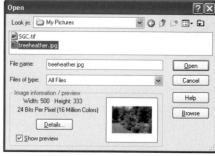

If you need to omit a background colour, select Layer, New Raster Layer. Set the background colour (e.g. white) and then select Edit, Paste, As Transparent Selection.

2 Choose Edit, Copy to copy the whole image, and then choose Windows, Image1 (ie the canvas).

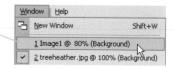

3 Select Edit, Paste, Paste As New Layer (or press Ctrl+L). The image will be placed on a raster layer in the centre.

When you paste the image, it will adopt the resolution of the canvas, so it may appear to change size. The image Title bar will show the magnification of the image, for example 80%. You may need to view the artwork at less than 100% so that you can see the whole image at once.

4 If the image is larger than the canvas, only the central part displays.

Resize image

1 Select the raster layer containing the image and click the Deformation tool to display the image frame and the handles.

2 Left click the middle of the image, and drag it so that one of the corners is in the required position.

3 Right click the corner opposite, and drag it to resize the image to the required size. Dragging with the right mouse button maintains the aspect ratio of the image.

4 You can left click and drag the image to reposition it more exactly. This does not affect the image quality.

Resize and Crop

If you make some changes, and then select Save, you will replace the original image file. Use Save As, and provide a different name for the modified image, to make sure you preserve the original version.

Using pixels for dimensions avoids problems when the image and the canvas have different resolutions.

Alternatively, you can change the image size before you copy it and paste it as a new layer.

1. Load the image file and choose Image, Resize.

2. Select Resample Using, to amend the size, and Lock Aspect Ratio, to maintain the proportions.

3. Choose the new image width, in pixels. The height is calculated automatically. Then click OK.

Crop image
If you want just part of the image, you can crop off the unnecessary parts.

1. Load the image file and select Image, Canvas Size.

2. Select Lock Aspect Ratio, if you want to crop proportionally.

Adjust the amount of cropping on the top, bottom and sides, to select just the required image content.

3. Specify the new width and height in pixels, establish the placement, and click OK to crop the image.

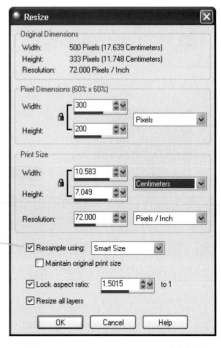

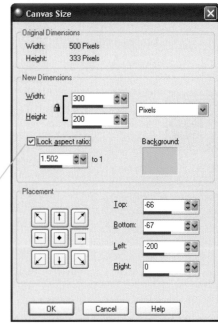

Vector layers

You have the option to create lines, shapes and text as raster or as vector. Choosing vector makes it easier to scale and manipulate the objects, but some functions operate only on raster forms, so Paint Shop Pro will convert the objects when you apply such tools.

Vector layers contain only vector objects (lines and shapes) and vector text. There are several tools that are specifically designed for vector operations.

- Text Tool

- Preset Shape Tool

- Pen Tool

- Object Selection Tool

Similar procedures are used for all of these vector items. For example, to change colours:

Choose the same colour for foreground and background, to create a single colour vector object, for example for monochrome text.

1. With the appropriate tool selected, click the Foreground box (shown here in darker green) and choose a new colour from the samples or from the colour wheel. Then click OK. This will set the line/outline colour of your shape or text.

Click the All Tools box to apply the colour change for all tools, vector and raster.

2. Click the Background colour (shown here in lighter green) to select a new colour as the Fill option.

3. For both foreground and background, you can select the gradient or pattern effects, or choose a texture, or select transparent colour.

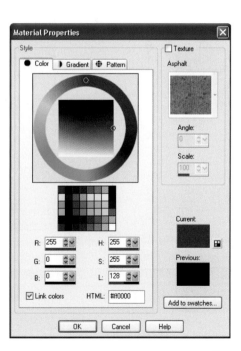

Draw preset shape

Clear the Retain Style box, or PSP Studio will disable the line style options and ignore your colour settings. Clear Anti-alias to get sharp edges to the lines and shapes.

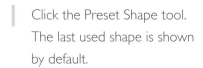
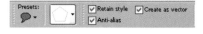

1 Click the Preset Shape tool. The last used shape is shown by default.

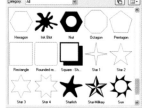

2 Click the arrow next to the preset shape to choose a different shape.

3 Select Create As Vector and clear Retain Style. Set the line and fill colours (see page 175), and choose the line style and width before starting to draw.

Save the artwork from time to time, so you don't have to start from the beginning if a problem arises.

4 Click and drag to create the shape, then release the mouse button. Hold down Shift as you drag, if you need to maintain proportions.

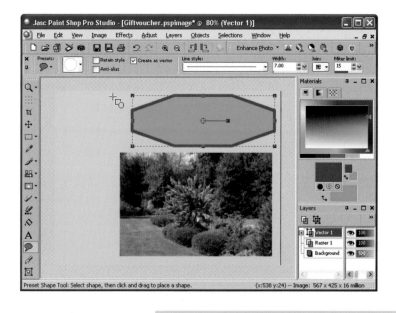

A new vector layer will be created above the current raster layer, or you can select an existing vector layer, to add the preset shape to that layer.

There's no loss of quality with vectors when you make any of these changes.

5 Click and drag the handles to adjust size, shape, rotation and position.

Enter text

If you create text as a vector, you can edit it, changing the words, font type, style and alignment.

1. Click the Text tool, and select Create As Vector. Set the font type and size, and select the Stroke and Fill colours and alignment, before adding text.

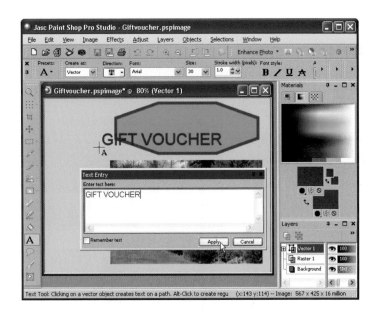

As with preset shapes, the text will be added to the current vector layer, or to a new vector layer if the current layer is raster.

Be sure to click outside any existing vector shape (or press Alt as you click), to prevent the text being wrapped around that shape.

2. Click on the canvas near where the text is to appear and type the words into the Text Entry box. Click Apply when complete.

3. Use the selection handles to move and resize the text, to position it for example within a preset shape.

If you right click away from the text you will lose the selection handles. To work with the text again, select the Object Selection tool (illustrated on page 175) and click within the text area.

4. Drag the rotation handle to turn text through any angle. Hold down the Shift key to rotate by increments of 15°, to make it easier to select an exact angle, vertical for example.

Edit artwork

If you have saved your artwork in the native .pspimage format, you can edit the properties of vector objects and change the contents of vector text.

1 Select the vector layer from the Layers palette and click on a vector object, shape or text, using the Object Selection tool.

If you choose an object directly from the vector palette, click the Object Selection tool to display the vector handles.

Select the object to move, rotate, shrink, expand or delete it. Edit the Vector Property box to change the line or fill colours and to adjust line thickness of the selected object.

2 Resize or reposition the object using the handles, or double click to display the Vector Property box and change colours and lines.

3 Click vector text using the Text tool to display the text entry box, and edit or replace the text or change font, style and size attributes. Only the highlighted section of the text will be changed.

Select the object and use the Windows style functions, e.g. Edit, Copy and Edit, Paste, to make a copy of the object.

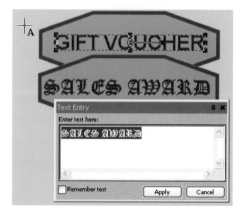

There are tools for manipulating raster images, or text and preset shapes created as raster.

1   Click the raster layer in the Layers palette and select the image using the Selection tool.

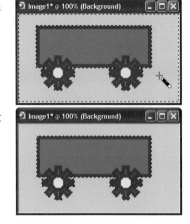

2   To select an irregular image, click in the background using the Magic Wand. Then choose Selections, Invert to reverse the selection.

3   Copy the image, or drag to move it, or select Image, Flip or Image, Mirror to reverse the image vertically or horizontally.

To select a coloured area, such as the background, click the arrow next to the Selection tool and choose the Magic Wand.

The Image, Resize command (see page 174) may be applied to the contents of the current raster layer, if you clear the Resize All Layers box, allowing you to expand or shrink an existing image.

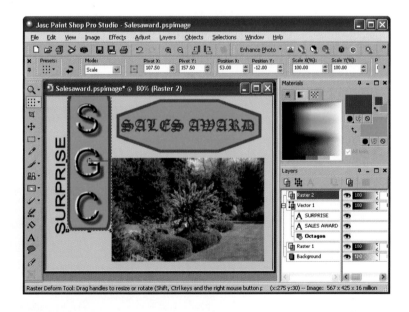

4   Click the Raster Deform Tool. Drag to reshape the image, or select Effects to apply one or more of the special actions available.

Transfer digital photographs

If you have a digital camera, the pictures you take are saved on a storage card. When you connect your camera (or a storage card reader), to your PC, you are able to download photographs from the card to your disk drive, where you can trim or enhance them with the image editor, then display or print them.

Copy all the images into a folder on your disk drive, to free up the storage card for additional photographs and to allow you to make changes to the pictures.

1 Connect the camera or reader, and Windows XP detects the device and asks you what action to take.

2 Choose to view pictures using suitable software, e.g. PSP Studio.

Some cameras and readers will appear on the PC as another disk drive. For the purposes of the CLAiT course, your tutor may provide photographs in a folder on the drive or the network. You can access these using the browser.

3 View images on the storage card or in the supplied folder, and double click an image to open it.

Annotate a photograph

1   Open a copy of the photograph that is stored on your disk drive. Always start with a copy of the original image, since progressive changes can reduce the quality of the image.

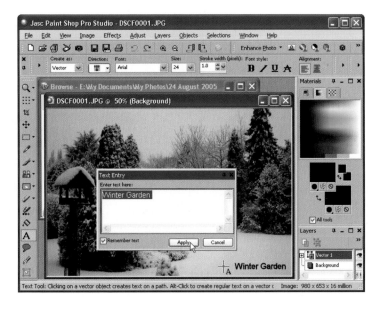

2   Click the Text tool, set the colours and styles, click on the image where you want words inserted, and type into the text box.

3   When you click Apply to insert the text, it appears as a new vector layer, above the original background layer.

4   Select Save As, and provide a new name for the modified image. You'll be notified that the image is being merged.

6. e-Image Creation   181

Change image resolution

The Image resolution (the pixels per inch or per centimetre) is the image size in pixels divided by the image dimensions (inches or centimetres).

Changing the image resolution will resize the image in one way or another. To illustrate the effects:

1   Load an image in PSP Studio, and select Image, Resize.

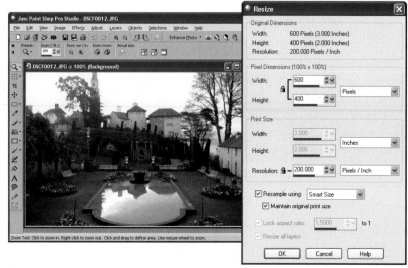

Since the image dimensions have been maintained unchanged, this reduces the number of pixels from 600x400 to 150x100.

2   Choose Sample Using Smart Size, and Maintain Original Print Size.

3   Change the Image Resolution from 200ppi to 50ppi.

When the image editor displays an image at 100%, it shows it at the resolution of the monitor, approximately 72-96ppi, depending on screen size. So low resolution images appear smaller than their actual dimensions.

When printed, the modified image will print at the original size, but it will be of much lower quality.

Changing image resolution this way gives a small file size taster version of the full image, perhaps for use as a photo album index.

4   Click OK to apply, and the resized image will be displayed in the image editor.

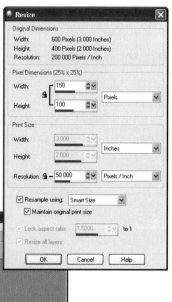

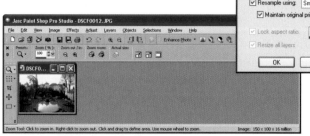

Print image

1 Open an image that you want to print, then select File, Print.

2 Click Printer to select the printer model. Choose Portrait or Landscape, position the image on the page, and click Print.

See Unit 4, covering Desktop Publishing for more details on colour printing.

Note that Print has an option to Fit To Page. Make sure it is deselected or it will change the size of your print.

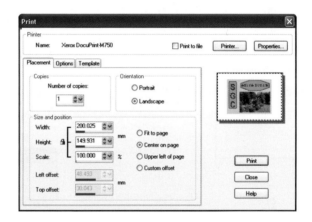

3 If you want to print an image in black and white, position the image then click the Options tab and select Greyscale.

The image editor gives you the option to print colour images in greyscale, or you can select Printer Properties and choose the Black and White option from there.

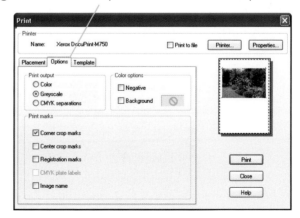

You'll be asked to write your name and centre number on the prints of images that you produce in the exercises or examinations. If you wish, you can use the image editor to add this information.

Print Layout is also used to position multiple images on a page, using pre-defined or custom templates.

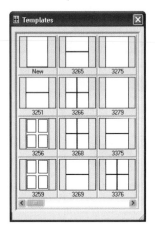

1 Open an image and select File, Print Layout.

2 Drag an image onto the page and position it (or click one of the positioning buttons).

3 Select the Text Field button, click on the page and type the annotation required.

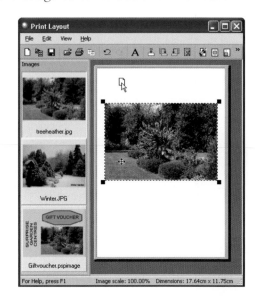

In Print Setup, you can choose Colour or Greyscale, select Crop Marks, change orientation, switch printers and set printer properties.

4 Select File, Print Setup or click the Print Setup button to change the layout or printer options.

5 Select File, Print or click the Print button to print the annotated image.

Unit 6 exercise

You are allowed two and a half hours to complete this exercise.

Scenario

You have been contracted by Surprise Gardens to create a front cover for their gift voucher scheme. The publicity manager has provided a layout of his preferred design.

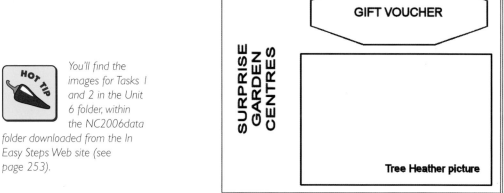

You'll find the images for Tasks 1 and 2 in the Unit 6 folder, within the NC2006data folder downloaded from the In Easy Steps Web site (see page 253).

You have also received a second design for a Sales Award recognition card, to be based on the gift voucher artwork.

Create a subfolder called Unit 6 in the CLAiT Coursework folder as a storage area to contain your worked copies.

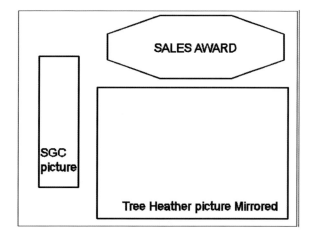

Image files Treeheather.jpg and SGC.tif and a photographs folder have also been provided.

Task 1

Before you begin this task, make
sure that you have the file
treeheather.jpg, and that you refer
to layout sketch one.

Images must not be distorted and must maintain their original proportions. Both text and images may be resized to suit the artwork, but must not touch the edge of the artwork or overlap any other items (other than the background). Also, they must have a transparent background (must allow the background colour of the artwork to be seen).

1. Create a new piece of artwork and set the size to be 20 cms wide and 15 cms high. Fill the background with light green.

2. Open the image treeheather.jpg and resize it so that it would occupy about 2/3rds the width of the artwork canvas. Insert it into the artwork and position it towards the lower right hand corner.

3. Above the image, create an octagon shape, with dark green outline and filled with bright green, and size this to be the same width as the picture, and to fill most of the height above the picture.

4. Within the octagon, type the following text as a single line and in a deep red colour:
GIFT VOUCHER
Size the text to fill the middle section of the octagon, without touching the sides.

5. Enter the following text on three lines and in a bright blue colour:
SURPRISE
GARDEN
CENTRES
Rotate the text 90° anticlockwise, and position it so it occupies most of the space to the left of the picture and octagon.

6 Save the artwork using a suitable file format, with the name Giftvoucher.

7 Print your artwork in colour, and on the printout write your name, your centre number and today's date.

Task 2

The Publicity manager has asked you to make the following changes to the giftvoucher artwork, to create a new sales award. Before you begin this task, make sure that you have the image file SGC.tif, and that you refer to layout sketch two.

1. Open the giftvoucher artwork.
2. Select the picture of the treeheather and flip it horizontally (mirror), retaining the position and size.
3. Edit the text in the octagon, using a fancy font such as Old English, to read as follows:
   SALES AWARD
   Size the text to fill the middle section of the octagon, without touching the sides.
4. Delete the SURPRISE GARDEN CENTRES text. Then open the image file SGC.tif, and insert it in place of that text.
5. Save the artwork using a suitable file format, with the name Salesaward.
6. Print your artwork in colour, and on the printout write your name, your centre number and today's date.

You'll find the images for Tasks 3 and 4 in the NC2006photos folder downloaded from the In Easy Steps Web site (see page 253).

Task 3

Before you begin this task make sure that you have access to a folder containing photograph files, including file DSCF0001.JPG.

1. Open the folder using the browser facility of your image editor, locate the file DSCF0001.JPG, and open this file.

2. Insert the following text, in black and positioned over the white snow area in the lower right corner:
   WINTER GARDEN
   Size the text to be easily read, but without obscuring the content of the picture (other than the plain snow area).
3. Save the picture using the file name Winter.jpg.
4. Print the modified picture in black and white, and on the printout write your name, your centre number and today's date.

Task 4

Before you begin this task make sure that you have access to a folder containing photograph files, including DSCF0012.JPG.

1. Open the folder using the browser facility of your image editor, locate the file DSCF0012.JPG, and open this file.
2. Change the image resolution of this file from the 200 pixels per inch to 50 pixels per inch, retaining the physical dimensions of the image.
3. Save the picture using the file name Wales.jpg.
4. Print the modified picture in colour, and on the printout write your name, your centre number and today's date.

Make sure that the image dimensions still show the initial values after you have changed the image resolution.

When you have completed this exercise, you should have the following printouts:
Giftvoucher
Salesaward
Winter
Wales

Web Page Creation

This unit uses FrontPage to develop a small web site. It includes importing, creating and formatting web pages and creating links. It develops an understanding of basic HTML concepts, web page navigation and browsing.

Covers

HTML Editors and Browsers | 190

FrontPage | 192

Build the web | 194

Open web pages | 196

Create links | 197

Save, Close, Reopen | 198

Create a new web page | 199

Format the page | 200

Insert an image | 202

Insert external links | 203

Check the links | 204

View in browser | 206

Hyperlinks view | 207

Printing web page and HTML | 208

Publish your web | 209

Unit 7 exercise | 210

Unit Seven

HTML Editors and Browsers

This unit provides you with the knowledge and understanding required to link existing web pages to a new web page to form a small web site. Web pages are defined using HTML (hypertext mark-up language). To create or modify pages, you need a text editor and to display the pages you need a browser.

The HTML Editor displays pages as you see them at the web site, with effects applied and images displayed and located in their proper positions. This is called WYSIWYG – What You See Is What You Get.

HTML Text Editor

There are several types of text editors that you could use. FrontPage or Dreamweaver, for example, are full function HTML editors. They will generate HTML code for you, and allow you to view the HTML statements in their raw form, or in the final format as they display at the web site. With these programs you can import and place text and image files, align the page items, adjust font sizes, styles and colours and format the web page. They also help you to insert links within the page or to other pages. These applications also provide additional facilities to automate the process of creating and maintaining the web site.

FrontPage also supports the use of XML (extensible markup language) which defines the structure of the data content of a web page. However, this is not a requirement for the CLAiT exercises.

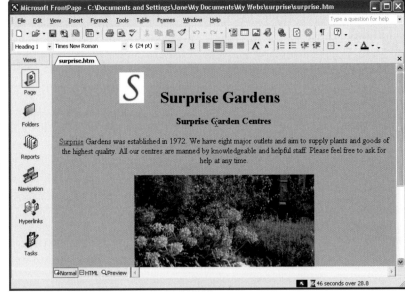

You could use a word processor such as Word or a desktop publishing application such as Publisher that can display and save files in the HTML format. These will provide the WYSIWYG view, and help generate valid HTML statements, but they do not support all the additional functions offered by the HTML editors. Since the HTML file format is plain text, you could use a plain text editor such as NotePad to create and modify the statements, but you would have to understand the HTML format completely. With plain text editors there would be no facilities for displaying text effects or images, or presenting them in the WYSIWYG view. There is also no means for validating the HTML statements. Plain text editors are used by experienced programmers who require full control over the way the HTML code is developed.

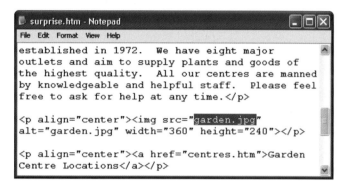

Using a browser to visit web sites, display web pages and navigate between web pages is covered in Unit 8 Online Communication.

For the purposes of this unit we will be using FrontPage to create, and modify the web site.

Web Page Browser

You need a web Browser such as Internet Explorer or Netscape to view, in their final form, the web pages that you have created. You should do this on your PC, before you send the HTML files to the web server that supports your web site. You and your web site visitors will also use a web Browser to view and navigate between web pages at the web site.

See page 206 for choosing a web browser to view your web site in FrontPage.

For the purposes of this unit, we will be using Microsoft Internet Explorer to display and link between web pages.

Publishing the web

The final step in creating a web site is to publish the web for all to see. You normally use an Internet Service Provider (ISP) who will provide the storage space and host the web site for you. Publishing is transferring the files from your PC to the web server. See page 209 for more information.

FrontPage

FrontPage allows you to create web pages and build web sites with all the functions and features of a professional web site. You can use the built-in functions, styles and themes to control the appearance, to save you handling the fine details, but you can also do things for yourself using specific HTML statements where necessary. When you have created the components of your web site, FrontPage helps you to set it up on a server, manage and monitor its use, and apply updates and changes.

If the Views Bar does not appear, select it from the View menu:

FrontPage views

The Views bar at the side of the FrontPage window lets you switch quickly between the different ways of looking at your web site contents.

Page view is used for creating and editing web pages. It lets you see them in the WYSIWYG format, as they would appear in a web browser. It lets you switch between Normal, HTML and Preview mode.

Folders view shows how the web content is organised, in the same style of view as Windows Explorer. You can manage the files and folders in this view.

Reports view lets you analyse the contents of your web. You can determine which files are not linked or out of date, you can calculate the total size of the files, and you can group the files.

Navigation view can be used to create, display and change the navigation structure of the web. It includes a folder side-bar, from which you can drag and drop pages into your structure.

Hyperlinks view shows the hyperlinks in your web, both internal and external. It shows graphically which links are working and which are broken.

Tasks view keeps a record of those tasks that are required to complete or maintain the website.

For the purposes of the New CLAiT course, you will only need to use Page, Folders and Hyperlinks views.

From the Windows Desktop select Start, All Programs, Microsoft FrontPage. The first time you open FrontPage, you may be presented with a blank page with the tab title New_Page_1.htm.

The New Page is just a default blank page.

From then on, FrontPage will remember the web folders you create, and will open in the most recently used folder.

For New CLAiT you are provided with a web site consisting of one or two web pages, plus a text file and an image file, with which to create an additional web page. These files should be contained within a folder.

Your web site

A web site is referred to simply as a web in FrontPage. It is comprised of a Home page, and optionally some secondary pages, each containing text, images and links. The links may be within the page or to other web pages and web sites.

To create the web site, you create the web site folder structure using FrontPage. You then import the existing pages and images. After this, you will insert a text and image file into a new page and format it to conform with the required style.

To create a new web site, select File, New, Page or web.

This displays the Task Pane, where you select New, Empty web. An empty web is a folder that contains only a standard set of subfolders.

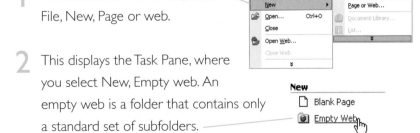

Notice how the mouse pointer becomes a hand when over a link to a function in FrontPage.

Build the web

The Empty web template assumes the location My Documents\ My webs, and suggests a name for the folder.

The location of the new web is displayed in a very small entry box, and you cannot see the full folder hierarchy. By default, FrontPage remembers the previously used web name and adds a consecutive number. Delete the suggested name and specify a new folder name. Note that OCR may ask you to put your own name on the folder.

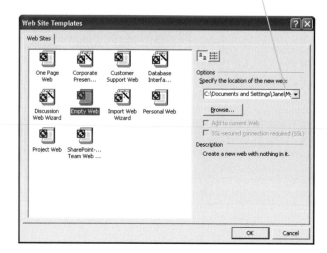

Check, and modify as necessary, the full location and name for the new web and click on OK. In Explorer view, the web folder shows the web symbol.

Jane Smith

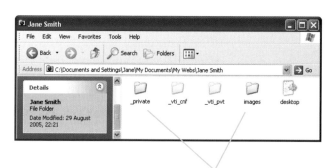

The two users folders are not needed in the CLAiT exercises. If you were creating a large web site, you should use them.

It contains two user folders, Private and Images. There are also two folders which are used by FrontPage and are normally hidden. To display them, select Tools, Folder Options, click the View tab and enable the setting Show hidden files and folders.

You have been supplied with two web pages. To use them in the new web, you must first import them.

By selecting all the files, you are sure that the associated image files are included in the web site and can be displayed where required in the web pages.

Note how the imported files have been added to the main web folder, not into the available subfolders.

Import pages

1 Select File, Import. The Import window will be empty, so click on Add File.

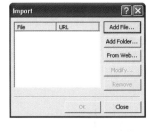

2 You will need to browse through the drive and folder structure to locate the files to add. To select all the files, click on the first and press and hold Shift as you click on the last. Then select Open.

3 Select any files not required and click Remove. Click OK to proceed.

4 The files are added to the web site. Change to the Folder view to see them.

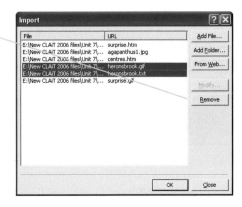

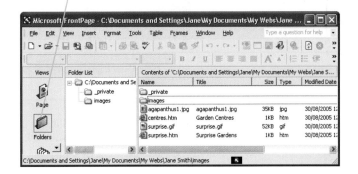

Open web pages

The web pages and associated images have been imported into the web site. To edit and amend the pages you must open them.

Each web page is a separate file. You can have just one page open, or all the pages open, but you have to open them individually as FrontPage does not allow you to open several files in one action.

1 Select File, Open or click on the Open button. FrontPage switches automatically to the Page view. Check to make sure that you are looking in the correct folder. Open all the necessary page files.

You can work with each page independently, but for some operations such as applying formats, it is easier to have them all open at the same time.

2 In Page view you will see each page with a separate tab, giving the file name. Each page also has its own Close button.

If you did not import the image, you will see a place holder on the web page. To import images see page 193.

3 Page view offers three ways to view each page. Normal view gives a WYSIWYG editing view. It allows normal word processing so you can add and amend text. You can apply format and layout changes and you can create Hyperlinks.

4 HTML view shows the underlying programming code in plain text form, so that you can see exactly what effects and actions have been defined.

The View selected is specific to each page.

5 Preview mode shows the page as it will appear in the browser. Animated effects are enabled and hyperlinks become live.

Create links

The home page is often given a standard name, such as Index.htm or Default.htm. For the purposes of New CLAiT, a meaningful name is used.

A web page is neither a page nor a screen – it is really just a file that can be viewed on the monitor. Depending on your monitor's resolution and the size of the page, you may see it all at once, or you may have to scroll sideways or down to see it all. You can create links to connect between pages, or between different locations on the same page. To create a link:

1 Highlight the text to use as a link. Select Insert, Hyperlink or click on the button to Insert Hyperlink

2 The Insert Hyperlink window shows the text used for the link. It is set to link to an existing file or web page, and displays the list of files in the current folder.

If you select the page to link, you will not get any typing errors that prevent the links from working.

Click here to place the link in the current document.

3 Select the page you wish to be linked and click OK. The linked text will be underlined and the mouse changes to a hand when on it. The page does not need to be open for the link to be created. To check the link, press Ctrl while you click, and the linked page will open. Use this method to check links before you save the page.

While the link text is still highlighted, switch to the HTML view to see the link code. The text is highlighted in both views.

```
<p align="center"><a href="centres.htm">Garden Centre Locations</a></p>
```

Save, Close, Reopen

Save

1 Each web page can be saved separately. Click on the Save button, or select File, Save. If you have several pages open, select File, Save All. You do not need to save the web, as such, as the web is the folder that contains the pages.

Close Web

2 You can close individual pages, or close the whole web. You will be prompted to save any pages or images that have not been saved previously.

If your next step is to create a new web, close the existing web before you close FrontPage. Otherwise you may find that you have nested your new web folder within an existing one. See page 194.

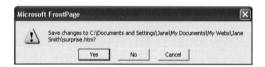

3 FrontPage remembers your last status. If you exited with a web open, it returns to that point. If you closed the web before you closed FrontPage, it will open with a blank new page.

The Open button in FrontPage allows you to select file or web. The button remembers your last action and displays that icon.

4 To reopen a web page, you can select from Recent Files. This opens the file and containing web folder. You can select from Recent webs to open the web without any pages.

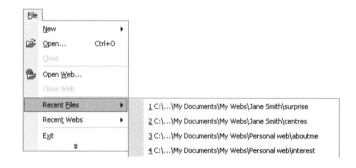

If you have the Task Pane open, you can select an existing file or web from there.

5 You can also use the Folder view to open web pages.

Create a new web page

The CLAiT exercise provides you with a text file, as well as the two web pages. You will use the text file to populate the new page.

1 With the existing web pages open, select New Page. It will be inserted as the next page, the tab showing the new_page_htm title.

2 To insert the text file data, select Insert, File. FrontPage opens the My Documents folder. The file should be located in the same folder as the existing web pages. You will need to navigate the folder structure to locate it.

Remember to save the page when you have inserted the text. You will be prompted for a file name.

The page tab will change to the new file name.

3 When you open the correct folder, the file may not be visible. You will need to change the Files of type window to look for Text Files. Select the file and click Open.

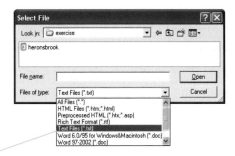

Try other conversion options when you insert the text to see the effect. Remember, you can always click Undo.

4 You will be asked to select a conversion option. The default is Formatted paragraphs. For the text style in most CLAiT exercises, the best option is Normal paragraphs.

5 Click on OK and the text will be inserted as separate paragraphs.

Format the page

Most professional publications and presentations have a defined style. A hierarchy of page heading, sub heading and paragraph or body text style will be chosen. Page headings will be formatted to a certain font size and style, subheadings to another, and body text to yet another. The web pages supplied by OCR will share such a style, and the new page must be formatted to conform.

The asterisk next to the tab heading indicates that the page has changed. When you close the web you will be prompted to save this file.

1 Click on the main heading of the home page. The formatting toolbar will display the style, font name and font size. It also indicates associated formatting such as bold and alignment.

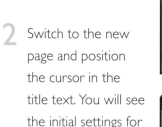

The Heading style is Times New Roman font, 6 (24pt) and bold. FrontPage uses such HTML styles rather than the standard Office styles, and the CLAiT exercises will specify formatting requirements in these terms.

2 Switch to the new page and position the cursor in the title text. You will see the initial settings for the imported text.

3 Click the down arrow, and select the font sizes to match the heading from the existing page (or apply the settings provided in the exercise). Add font effects and alignment settings, e.g. bold and centred.

You can use the Format Painter to copy the style from one page to another. Click on the text with the style to copy, select the Format brush and click on the new text to apply the format.

4 Repeat the same procedure to apply the formats for subheadings and body text on the new page. Select the secondary heading or body text from a supplied page to confirm the format style, before you apply it to the new page.

5 Line spacing is controlled as in normal word processing.

Web pages should be attractive, so a variety of layouts and alignments are frequently used.

6 The standard alignment tools work with text and with images. Centred items will remain centred on the display, even if you change the screen resolution or the window size.

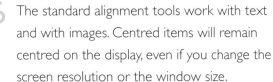

7 To change the background colour of the current page, select Format, Background. Notice the small Fill symbol on the command.

8 Select the Background colour. You may wish to select from More Colours.

It is important to use a colour that allows the text to be clearly visible. Many of the standard colours are primary colours – a paler shade may be more appropriate.

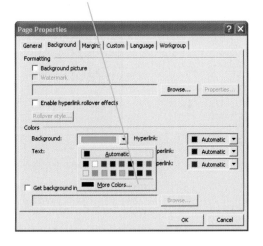

Themes can be customised to implement a house style. However, these are not needed in the CLAiT exercises.

9 FrontPage provides Themes to help you use effective and consistent colouring and layout on your web. The Theme can be applied to all or selected pages.

Insert an image

Press Enter if needed to create a blank line where you want to insert the image.

1 Position the cursor where you want to place the picture and select Insert, Picture, From File.

When you import an image or .htm file, a copy is added to your web and the original stays in the source folder.

2 FrontPage remembers any previous folder used for image files, so you may need to browse the folders to find the correct one. To help you select the image, select Views from the Picture window and pick Preview. Choose the file and click Insert.

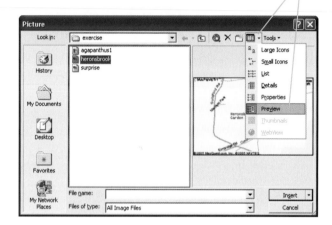

You will be prompted to save any embedded image files, when you save the page.

3 The image will appear at the cursor position. To complete the positioning, click the image and then click the appropriate alignment button, e.g. centre.

If the image is embedded in a section of text, right click the image and select Picture Properties, then click the wrapping style required.

Insert external links

1 The link to the external web page uses the same mechanism as a link to an internal web page. Select the text to be linked. Click Insert Hyperlink. See page 197.

2 The external URL address must be typed in to the Address bar. FrontPage inserts the http:// prefix as you type www. Click OK to insert.

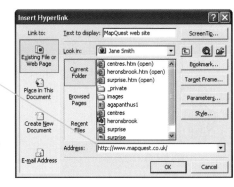

3 When you use Ctrl and click to test the link, the web site will open in FrontPage, with the tab heading [Default Page].

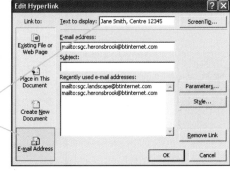

4 To insert a link to an e-mail address, select the text and click Insert Hyperlink. The selected text is placed in the Text to display box. Select the E-mail Address button. When you type the e-mail address FrontPage inserts the 'mailto:' prefix. Click OK to complete the process. Note, you cannot check this link using Ctrl and click.

Check the links

You can check the hypertext links by using Ctrl and click, as shown on page 197. This method is used in Normal page view. It is a quick way to verify most links as you create them, but cannot be used for e-mail links.

Normal HTML Preview

When you check the links in Preview, the linked page opens on the same page tab, which may cause confusion. Switch back to Normal view to see the pages on their correct page tab.

When you have created several links, and saved the pages, check them using the Preview facility. Select the button at the bottom of the screen. You are still running FrontPage, but are using some of the code from Internet Explorer. The advantage is that you are able to view any animated images, and the links are live.

Click any link and it loads the linked page onto the same page tab. To check external links you must be connected to the Internet.

Reports

The Report facility gives an overview of the web site, providing statistics, name and sizes of files and the status of hyperlinks. The Site Summary is the main view, individual topics can be viewed in detail. Click the button to open the main report.

Reports

The specific items you need to check on the Report are Hyperlinks, Unverified and Broken hyperlinks.

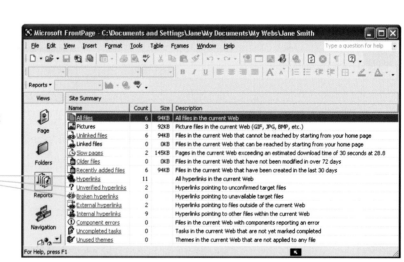

Name	Count	Size	Description
All files	6	94KB	All files in the current Web
Pictures	3	92KB	Picture files in the current Web (GIF, JPG, BMP, etc.)
Unlinked files	6	94KB	Files in the current Web that cannot be reached by starting from your home page
Linked files	0	0KB	Files in the current Web that can be reached by starting from your home page
Slow pages	2	145KB	Pages in the current Web exceeding an estimated download time of 30 seconds at 28.8
Older files	0	0KB	Files in the current Web that have not been modified in over 72 days
Recently added files	6	94KB	Files in the current Web that have been created in the last 30 days
Hyperlinks	11		All hyperlinks in the current Web
Unverified hyperlinks	2		Hyperlinks pointing to unconfirmed target files
Broken hyperlinks	0		Hyperlinks pointing to unavailable target files
External hyperlinks	2		Hyperlinks pointing to files outside of the current Web
Internal hyperlinks	9		Hyperlinks pointing to other files within the current Web
Component errors	0		Files in the current Web with components reporting an error
Uncompleted tasks	0		Tasks in the current Web that are not yet marked completed
Unused themes	0		Themes in the current Web that are not applied to any file

Unverified links occur if you mistype a URL, or if you change file names or locations after the page was created.

Always use the FrontPage Folder view if you need to change file locations as the links are automatically updated.

1 Click on Unverified hyperlinks in the Name column to see the itemised list of problems. You will be asked if you wish the links verified.

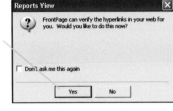

2 Click Yes to check the hyperlinks if you are connected to the Internet. To perform the check later, you can use the Verify Hyperlink button on the Reports toolbar.

3 FrontPage checks the links and creates a new report. The Status bar shows the updated summary. One link is verified; the broken link is created by a mistyped URL.

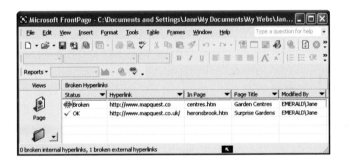

4 To amend the hyperlink, right click the incorrect URL and select Edit Hyperlink. You can Edit Page to return to the original location of the link. When you type the corrected name, FrontPage automatically checks again. The Report will be updated. Press F5 (Refresh), or select View, Refresh to update the details on the Status bar.

View in browser

See page 204 for checking links in Preview mode.

The page Preview mode lets you view your web pages in a simulated browser view. You need to check the pages in full browser mode, using your default browser and other browsers that your visitors might employ, to ensure that everything works as expected.

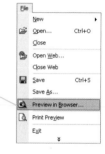

 You can use the Preview in Browser button on the toolbar but to access all the options, you need to select File, Preview in Browser.

You will need to save the pages before you can view them in the browser.

2 The dialog box lists available browsers. Select the Add button to include a browser on your PC that is not currently listed.

3 Click Preview and a copy of the selected browser is loaded, allowing use of the full browser functions, including the Back and Forward buttons.

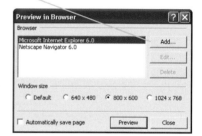

Use the different browsers and resolutions to see how the pages might appear to visitors with different facilities.

To return to FrontPage, click the Close button on the browser title bar.

Hyperlinks view

1. The Hyperlinks view shows the links created, both internal and external. Select each page in turn to see the associated links.

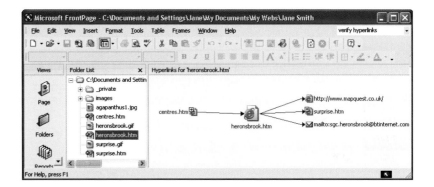

2. You can right click a hyperlink to verify it. Broken links are clearly identified.

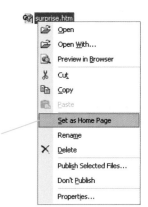

3. Hyperlinks view can be used to define the home page for your web site. Right click the main page, surprise.htm in the Folder List and select Set as Home Page. This changes its name to index.htm and updates all links to the page.

The name of the page in the Folder List may not change immediately.

For the CLAiT exercise specifying the Home Page in this way is not required.

When you visit a web site, you normally specify the name of the web site without any page names. The browser will search through a list of standard names such as index. htm, default.htm, index.html and default.html. It will display the first match. If you name your Home page differently, your web site may not be found.

URLs are case sensitive, so it is also important to use a consistent rule, to name all your web pages and files. The best choice it to always use lower case.

Printing web page and HTML

1 With your web pages open, select Preview in Browser. The size of the browser window or the screen resolution won't affect the printout, so any setting is OK.

2 Use Page Setup and Print Preview in the browser to make sure that there are no problems with the document.

3 The printed page will normally print without the background fill colour. It will show the page title in the header area, and the file source information in the footer area.

The print of the HTML source code provides proof of the hyperlinks and the use of background colour.

4 Switch to the HTML view and select File Print Preview to see the layout, then select Print to produce the printout.

5 You can also print the HTML code from the browser window. Select View, Source. It will open in a copy of NotePad, the plain text editor, from where you can select File, Print.

Publish your web

To make your web available to visitors on the Internet, you must copy all the files and folders to the web server managed by your Internet Service Provider (ISP). The method used to publish your web depends on whether your ISP offers a web server with FrontPage Server Extensions services installed. The server extensions are not essential, but with them available you can take advantage of extra functions such as forms and counters, and use FrontPage to maintain your files and hyperlinks. Each time you publish the web, FrontPage compares the files on your local computer to the files on the web server. If you move a file in your web on the hard disk, FrontPage will update and correct any hyperlinks to it, and then make the same corrections to the web server files, the next time you publish the web. FrontPage uses HTTP (Hypertext Transfer Protocol) to transfer the files.

If your ISP does not support the server extensions, your web must be published using FTP (File Transfer Protocol) and you will have to manage the file and hyperlink changes yourself.

1 Open the web and click the Publish button (or select File, Publish web) to start the process.

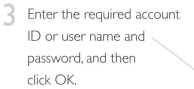

2 Enter the web site URL or the FTP address for the web server providing your web space.

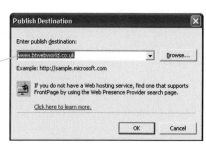

3 Enter the required account ID or user name and password, and then click OK.

4 FrontPage connects to the Internet and transfers the files

Unit 7 exercise

You are allowed two and a half hours to complete this exercise.

Scenario

You are working in the Promotion Department of 'Surprise Gardens'. Your job is to help develop the company web pages. Your manager has two pages prepared, which need to be linked. These are the files provided:

surprise.htm	the 'Surprise Gardens' homepage.
centres.htm	a page listing the individual centres.
surprise.gif	the image file for the logo on all web pages.
agapanthus1.jpg	the image used in the surprise.htm web page.
heronsbrook.txt	content for the 'Heronsbrook' page (Task 2).
heronsbrook.gif	picture for the 'Heronsbrook' page (Task 2).

The files needed for this exercise are in Unit 7 of NC2006data which can be downloaded from the In Easy Steps web site (see page 253).

Task 1

1. Create a folder to contain the web pages and images that you will amend or create. Name/rename this folder with your own name.

2. Import the web pages provided into your new folder, along with the image files required for these web pages.

Create a subfolder in the CLAiT Coursework folder to store your worked answers for this exercise.

3. Open your web page editor and open the supplied web page surprise.htm.

4. Create a link in the surprise.htm page as follows:

Text to be linked:	Garden Centre Locations
Link to:	centres.htm

   Enter your name and exam centre number after the text:
   Updated by ....

5. Save the amended surprise.htm page.

6. Open the centres.htm web page and create a link at the bottom of the page, as follows:

Text to be linked:	Surprise Gardens
Link to:	surprise.htm

   Enter your name and exam centre number after the text:
   Updated by.... Save the amended centres.htm page.

7. Test the links on each of these pages.

The text and the graphic files will also be found in the Unit 7 folder of NC2006data.

You have been asked to make a new page with location information for one of the centres. The new page must be formatted according to the company's web design policy as shown in the diagram.

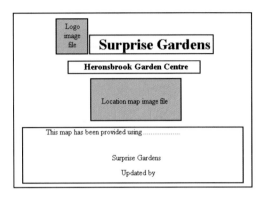

Task 2

1. Create a new page and insert the text file heronsbrook.txt. Enter your name and exam centre number after the text: Updated by:

2. Format the heading text Surprise Gardens as Times New Roman, HTML size 6 (24 point), bold.
   Format the subheading text Heronsbrook Garden Centre as Times New Roman, HTML size 4 (14 point), bold.
   Format all other text as Times New Roman, HTML size 3 (12 point), regular.
   Ensure that each paragraph is separated by a clear linespace.

3. Format all the text to be centre-aligned on the page.
   Embolden the text MapQuest web site.
   Italicise the text "Please make it soon".

4. The page must include the Surprise gardens logo. Import the graphic surprise.gif and position it just left of the heading.

5. Import the graphic heronsbrook.gif and position it below the text 'Heronsbrook Garden Centre', and above the text 'This map has been provided'.
   Make sure that the graphic is centre-aligned on the page.

Task 3

1. The new page should link back to the 'Surprise Gardens' homepage. Create a link in the new page as follows:

Text to be linked:	Surprise Gardens
Link to:	surprise.htm

   Save the new page as heronsbrook.htm.

2. The 'Centres' page should have a link to the new page. In the centres.htm page, locate the text Heronsbrook.
   Link this text to your newly created page, heronsbrook.htm.
   Save the amended centre.htm page.
   Load all the pages into the browser and test the new links.

3. Change the background colour of the surprise.htm page ensuring that it is different from the text colour.
   Save the amended surprise.htm page to disk.

Some links on the 'Heronsbrook' web page need completing.

Task 4

1. Create an external link in the heronsbrook.htm page as follows:

Text to be linked:	MapQuest web site
External link to:	www.mapquest.co.uk

   Save the amended surprise.htm page.

2. Create an e-mail link in the heronsbrook.htm page as follows:

Text to be linked:	Your name and exam centre number
External link to:	sgc.heronsbrook@btinternet.com

   Save the amended heronsbrook.htm page.

3. Load the surprise.htm page into the browser, print a copy.
   Load the centres.htm page into the browser, print a copy.
   Load your new page into the browser and print a copy.
   Print a copy of the HTML code used for each of the 3 pages.

4. Close each document and exit the application.

You should have six printed pages when you have finished the exercise.

Online Communication

This unit covers the two basics of electronic communication: e-mail and the Internet. The e-mail component includes sending, receiving, forwarding mail, using attachments, the address book and checking for viruses. The Internet element includes searching the web and managing the results.

Covers

E-mail and the Internet | 214

Internet security | 216

Viruses | 217

Start Outlook Express | 218

Receive e-mail | 220

The address book | 221

Receive attachments | 223

Create e-mail | 225

Send, reply and forward | 227

Send an attachment | 230

Organise your mail | 231

Print your e-mail | 232

The World Wide Web | 233

Search engines | 235

Save images and text | 238

Manage web addresses | 240

Printing web pages | 241

Unit 8 exercise | 242

Unit Eight

E-mail and the Internet

For the purpose of the New CLAiT course, electronic communication can be divided into two categories – communication between individuals and communication to a general audience. E-mail is used to send information between friends, family, business contacts etc., in other words, between individuals. The Internet, or World Wide Web is used to make information available to anyone.

E-mail

E-mail stands for electronic mail. It uses telephone and computer connections and can be extremely swift and inexpensive. You can communicate with someone the other side of the world within minutes, at a fraction of the cost of an international telephone call, and much faster than regular mail.

The application we are using for e-mail is Outlook Express, which has e-mail as its main function. It is also possible to use Outlook

– the e-mail part of Outlook is very similar to Outlook Express, as the name would suggest. However, Outlook is also a time management system. It includes a calendar, notes, messages and tasks. It has greater function than needed for this course but can be used in the same way to complete the exercises.

Outlook Express is a PC based e-mail system. This means that you can type and save e-mail messages off-line. When you are ready, connect to your Internet Service Provider (ISP) and send the messages. While you are connected, the computer checks for messages that are held for you by your ISP, and downloads them to your computer. You can then disconnect and read them at your leisure. All of this usually only takes a few minutes.

Some e-mail systems are web based, Hotmail for example. You must first connect, then read and create e-mail whilst you are connected. The great advantage of web-based e-mail is that you can read and send e-mail from anywhere in the world. The messages are stored on the ISP's computer, so you are not using your own storage space.

One way to make information available on the web is to create your own web pages and upload them to a host computer. Creating your own web pages is covered in Unit 7. (see pages 199-203).

The Internet

The Internet is an interwoven network of computers, or a web, all connected via telephones and satellites. The information that is held on the web is provided by organisations, companies, governments and individuals.

To search for information on the Internet you need to use a browser. There are other browsers in common use, such as Netscape and Opera, but we are going to use Microsoft's Internet Explorer which comes with all versions of Windows.

If you right click the Dial Up connection, you can select to show the connection icon in the notification area (system tray). When you hover the mouse over the icon, you will see your connection rate. You can also use this icon when you want to disconnect.

The connection

To browse the Internet or to send and receive e-mail, you must be signed on to your ISP. The speed of your connection will affect the rate at which you receive information, whether it is e-mail, possibly with attachments, or web pages. Cable or broadband (ADSL) connections provide the best rates available. To view your connection rate, select My Network Places, then right click and select Properties. Then double click your Dial Up connection. This will show the Status, Duration and speed of your connection.

Internet security

Connecting to the Internet, for either surfing or for e-mail purposes, can leave your computer open to potentially harmful viruses, or attack by intruders who may try to access data on your computer. It is very important therefore, to install, regularly update and use the preventative measures that are available.

Firewall software

Windows XP operating system comes with firewall software (which is automatically switched on). Other suppliers include ZoneAlarm and Norton's Utilities.

This security measure monitors and restricts communication between your computer and others on the Internet. It helps to prevent unauthorised access to your computer. It blocks unauthorised requests for access but allows you to create exceptions for programs such as games and messaging services.

Phishing (pronounced fishing) is the sending of e-mail to an address, falsely claiming to be from a legitimate source, in an attempt to trick the receiver into giving away private information. The e-mail directs the user to a web site which is bogus but looks genuine, where you are asked to update information such as bank or credit card details and passwords. The only protection is common sense.

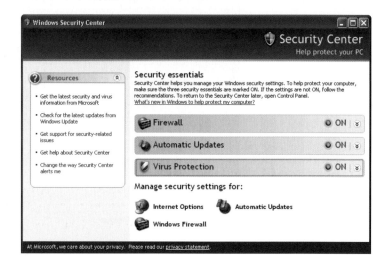

Never reply to e-mail that you think may be suspect, and never use the links provided in the e-mail. Always type in the web address you would normally use.

Popup blockers

When you surf the Internet, you will visit sites that are very keen to advertise and attract your attention. They do this by opening small windows that pop into view and display eye-catching graphics. They are generally considered an irritation and may affect productivity and efficiency. Standard security software is designed to block these windows.

Select Start, Control Panel and click on Security Center to view and if required, change the settings.

Windows updates

Keeping your operating system up-to-date will also help to maintain your system's security. Set your options to allow Automatic updates if you have an 'always on' Internet connection.

Viruses

There are several types of malicious programs that can cause damage to your computer. The virus attaches itself to a program or file so it can spread from one computer to another. A virus is usually attached to an executable file (a program that can be run) but it cannot infect your computer if you do not open or run it.

A Worm is similar to a virus, but unlike a virus, it has the ability to travel unaided, by taking advantage of file or information transport features on your system. It is able to broadcast itself, so your computer could send out hundreds of copies of the worm, infecting other computers and causing computers and web servers to stop responding.

Your computer should be automatically checked by the antivirus software as you work, surf the Internet and access and download e-mails and attachments. You can instigate a scan of your PC if you feel it necessary, or if you want to scan an individual attachment. To scan for viruses:

1 Click Start, All Programs and locate your antivirus software. It may also be accessible from the Notification area on the Desktop.

2 Select the drive or drives to check. If you have saved an attachment to floppy disk and only want to check the attachment, just select the A: \ drive and click Go.

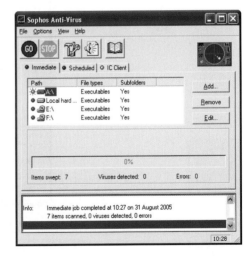

3 The drive will be scanned and a status report displayed when the job completes.

Start Outlook Express

Outlook Express is a standard entry in the Windows Start menu. Single click to select and open it. The default window that opens is the main view of the application. It provides access to all the activities.

Outlook Express is also included in the Quick Launch bar (if you have this enabled on the task bar), so it is quickly and readily available.

1 If you are using a modem to connect to the Internet, Outlook Express normally starts up Off-line. When you press Send and Receive it will dial up to your ISP.

2 The left pane shows the default view of Outlook Express, with the folder list and Contacts list.

To see the Toolbars and Status bar, select View from the menu bar and tick the bars you want.

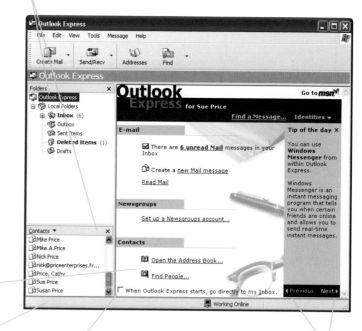

You can click on any underlined item to go to that activity.

The status bar will tell you if you are in the Online mode.

3 Tick this box to go straight to the Inbox view and bypass this window.

4 You can scroll through Tip of the day to get more useful suggestions.

The Outlook Express Folders

It is important to understand the function of each folder in Outlook Express.

The Inbox – e-mail is downloaded automatically into this folder. It remains here until you read, file or delete it.

To set your preferences for automatic Send/ Receive, select Tools, Options, and the General tab.

The Outbox – when you have created your messages, click on Send. The messages will be transferred to the Outbox and will remain there until you select Send/Receive. If you are working on-line, you can set Outlook Express to perform a Send/Receive automatically at set frequencies. If you are working off-line, select Send/Receive when you have finished and the messages will disappear from the Outbox.

To expand subfolders, click on the + symbol. To collapse subfolders click on the - symbol.

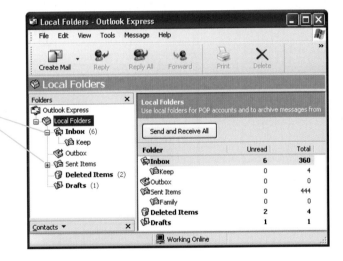

To view the contents of any folder, just click on the folder name in the Folders pane.

Sent Items – a copy of all the e-mail you have sent is normally transferred to the Sent Items folder.

Deleted Items – when you delete messages, they are sent to this folder, but will remain there until you empty the folder.

In business environments, or where computer disk storage is at a premium, you may find that a copy of the message is not automatically put in the Sent items. Select Tools, Options and the Sent tab to check.

Drafts – this is the folder where you can store e-mail that you have created, but not completed, or messages that you do not wish to send at this point.

You can also create your own folders and subfolders (see page 231).

Receive e-mail

The Inbox

When you connect to your ISP, either automatically or by pressing Send/Receive, any messages you have will arrive in the Inbox.

1 You can select the Inbox by clicking in the Folder list. This shows you at a glance how many messages are waiting to be read.

2 The right pane lists the messages that have arrived. Closed envelopes indicate unread messages, also indicated by the bold type. Once read, the envelope shows as open.

You don't have to read unsolicited messages or junk mail if you don't want to. Just select them and press delete.

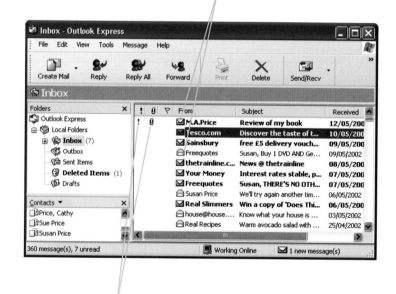

You can customise your view of the Inbox to include a preview pane. It shows the first few lines of the selected message. In effect, this opens the message automatically. This means that you cannot screen your messages, especially for viruses, before you open them.

3 The paper clip indicates that this e-mail has an attachment. The exclamation mark shows that the sender has marked it as priority.

For more information on attachments see page 223.

4 The status bar shows how many messages are in the Inbox, and that there is one new message. You will normally get an audible indication that you have a new message.

5 Double click the message to open it.

The Address Book

The generic format of an e-mail address is:

$$userid@mailserveraddress$$

Some addresses are case sensitive, so type the e-mail address exactly as given.

user name/number

name of the computer
storing the user's e-mail

required separator
(pronounced 'at')

To add an address to your Address Book:

1 Open the message. Click on the name of the sender. Right click and select Add to Address Book.

2 The contact will be added to your Address Book, and the new entry will appear in the contacts list without any further prompting.

As with many activities in Microsoft Office there is more than one way to add an address to the address book. Just use the method that suits you best.

3 If the contact already exists, you will get a message to that effect.

4 You can add the sender's name to the Address Book from the message entry in the Inbox. Right click the message and select to Add Sender.

5 In both these methods, only the e-mail address is added to the Address Book, no other details are completed. Some contacts have more than one e-mail address. To see the e-mail address used, select Properties.

To add an address manually, or to edit and complete details in the address book:

1 Click the Addresses button on the toolbar, visible whichever folder is selected.

Addresses

If you use the automated ways of adding a contact, you can avoid mistyping the address.

2 Select New to add a new address. To change an existing entry, select the contact and click Properties.

3 Complete the details. You will see that you can add Home, Business and other information. Type in the e-mail address and click Add. The address will be moved to the lower pane and the words Default E-Mail added.

You can also use the Properties button in the Select Recipients window to add or amend details for a contact.

4 The information in the Display box is filled in automatically, and is used in the Contacts pane. You can choose to have surname first if you wish.

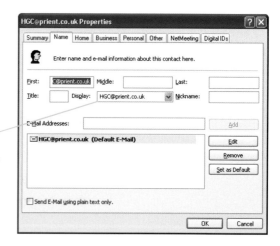

If your contact has more than one address, you can decide which to set as the default.

If you need to send plain text messages only, click the box in the bottom left corner. Business systems and office environments often prefer to receive plain text messages.

5 To print the Address Book entry, complete the details and click OK to save and close the Properties window. With the contact selected in the Address Book, click on Print or select File, Print.

Receive attachments

An attachment can be a document, an image, a spreadsheet or other type of file. An attachment is indicated on the e-mail by the paper clip symbol.

For the New CLAiT exercise you must be able to receive, open, save, file, print and forward attachments. On this page we look at receiving, opening and printing.

Open the message. You will see the name, the type, (.doc, .xls, .jpg etc.) and the size of the attachment.

You might wish to look at the file before you print to see how many pages it will use.

Attachments can contain viruses. You should make sure that you have an up-to-date virus checking program running on your computer, and only open e-mail and attachments if you are sure of the source. See page 217.

Select the attachment and right click. From this menu you could choose to print. You will not need to open the attachment to print.

You can select to open the attachment from this menu or you can double click on the name. In either case you could be prompted with a warning, depending on the file type.

If the attached file is an image file, such as a .jpg or .tif file, the warning message may not appear.

...cont'd

A copy of the attachment will remain with the original e-mail in the Inbox.

4 To be able to open the attachment, the file type must be registered on your system. This means it will have an associated application. See page 24 for more detail.

5 By preference you should save the attachment to disk. This will give you an opportunity to check out the file for viruses before processing it. You will see in the Warning message that the default is to save the file this way.

6 Select OK to save the file to disk, and you will be presented with the My Documents folder. You can browse to select a different folder or drive, and accept or modify the file name, although you must retain the file type, e.g. .htm.

7 A more direct way of saving an attachment is to select from the menu, File, Save Attachments.

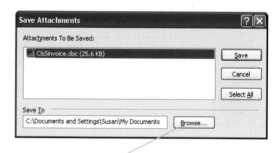

To open the attachment, minimise or close Outlook Express and select Start, My Documents (if you have saved the file to My Documents). Locate the file and double click on the file icon to open the attachment. It will open in its associated program.

8 The Save Attachments window lists files attached to the message, and allows you to browse the folders to select where you wish to save.

9 Click OK when you have selected the folder. You will then be able to confirm the file name and save the attachment.

Create e-mail

There are two easy ways to create a new e-mail.

1 Double click the name of the addressee in the Contacts pane. This will take you to the New Message window with the To: box automatically completed.

When you complete the Subject bar the e-mail Title bar changes from New Message to the subject. In effect, the subject becomes the file name.

2 Alternatively you can click on the Create Mail button in the Toolbar. This also brings you to the New Message window. With either method, you will see that the From box has been filled in with your e-mail address. If you have more than one address, click the down arrow in the From bar and select which identity to use.

There is more information on selecting recipients later in the unit when we look at sending copies of e-mail. See page 227.

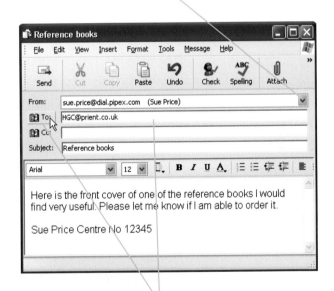

When you type in the recipient's address, you must make sure to get it absolutely correct including all symbols such as @ and underscores.

3 With this method, you will need to complete the To: box. You can type in the address yourself, or click on the word To: which becomes a button when you pass the mouse over it. Click it to open the Select Recipients window for you to choose one or several recipients. See page 226.

4 With the Select Recipient window open, double click the name, or select the name and click on the To: button. Do this for each main recipient; you can have several.

This uses the Address Book. For more information on using and managing addresses, see page 221.

5 You can use the Cc: box to send carbon or courtesy copies to others. Select the name and click the Cc: box.

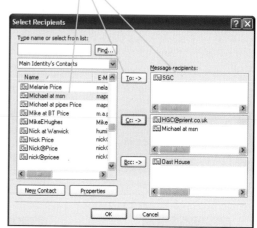

Everyone can see the main and copied recipients. Only the sender and the receiver themselves know who gets the Bcc.

6 The Bcc: box means a blind (or hidden) carbon copy.

7 With your e-mail recipients selected, click on OK.

8 Complete the Subject box. If you leave this blank, you'll get a warning that there's no subject, when the message is sent.

To de-select a name in the recipient's box, just select it and press delete.

9 Click in the main typing area and type in your message. The spell check facility is available, as well as the normal editing tools.

10 You will see above the typing area the usual text formatting bar so that you can use bold, underline etc. in your message. You can also choose to apply Stationery effects when you initially create the message, although not everyone can see this formatting when they receive the message.

Although you can send formatted text and stationery, it is not required by CLAiT.

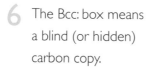

Send, reply and forward

If you are unable to complete your e-mail message, and wish to save but not send, click File, Save. The message will be put in the Drafts folder. To open it, single click on the Drafts folder in the folder pane. The message will appear listed on the right. Double click the message, to open it and continue.

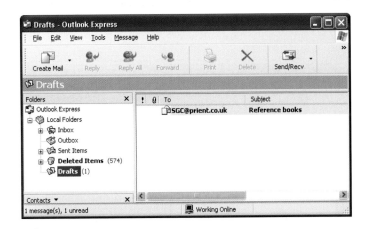

2 When you have completed the message you can decide whether to send now or later. To send now, select the Send button. If you are on-line the message will be sent immediately. If you are off-line, the message will be placed in the Outbox where it will remain until you next connect.

Check that a copy of the message will be put in the Sent Items folder. See the Hot Tip at the foot of page 219. At the end of the exercise, you will be required to print a copy of all the messages sent.

3 You can decide to Send Later. This facility allows you to write all your e-mails before you connect. When you do connect, all the mail is sent at once.

4 If you are working off-line, and there are messages in the Outbox, click Send/Receive to connect and send. The Outbox will empty.

Reply

Replying to an e-mail is probably the easiest and quickest way to communicate.

1   Select the message and click on Reply. If there were several recipients you can choose Reply All.

2   You will see that the message header has been completed for you. Re: has been inserted in the Subject box.

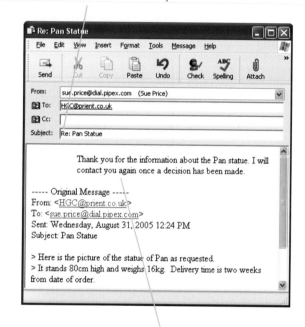

3   The first lines of the message area start off blank for you to insert your response.

4   The original message is part of the reply. You can delete the text if you wish but it is usual to leave it there to provide a context for the reply. The attachment, however, will be dropped. When you have completed your reply, click Send.

Forward

Forwarding a message works in a similar fashion as replying to a message.

1 Select the e-mail from the Inbox list and click on the Forward button. Alternatively, from the menu you can select Message, Forward.

2 You must complete the To: box yourself. You can type in the address, or click on the To: and invoke the address book. Add Cc entries as required.

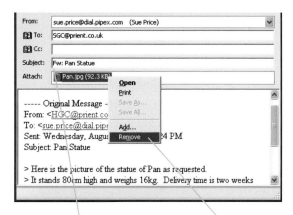

For the CLAiT exercise, a printed copy of the Forwarded message will be required. It must include Fw: in the Subject box.

3 This time the Subject box contains Fw: in front of the subject. The attachment and the original message are included.

4 You may decide that it is inappropriate to include the attachment. Select the attachment and right click. You now have the option to remove it.

5 Outlook Express modifies the e-mail icons so you can understand the status of the messages.

Unread   Reply

Read   Forward

Send an attachment

1 Create your e-mail and fill in the details on the message header.

2 Select Insert Attachment or click on the Attach button. This will open the Insert Attachment window for you to select a file.

For the New CLAiT exercise, you will use the Internet to find a specific image file and save it for later use. It is this file that you will need to attach to your e-mail.

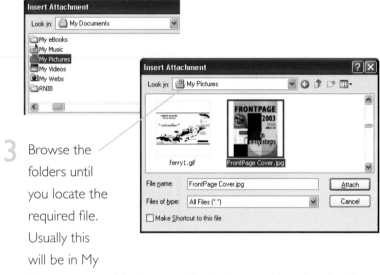

3 Browse the folders until you locate the required file. Usually this will be in My Documents or My Pictures. Notice that at this point the Files of type box is set to look for all files. With folders containing a large number of files, select the down arrow on the box and choose a file type to act as a filter.

When you send an attachment, consider the size of the file. If your recipient has a slow connection, it can take a long time to download the file.

4 Click the Attach button. You will return to your message, and the header section will now include an attachment with file type indicator and size.

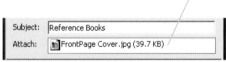

Using Zip files is not a New CLAiT requirement.

For large files, Windows XP has a Zip compression facility.

Organise your mail

Your Inbox, like any other storage medium, needs to be monitored and organised. After you have read your e-mail, you have to decide what course of action to take.

1 To delete messages, just select them and press the delete key or click the delete button.

2 You can drag and drop messages into the Deleted Items folder.

Messages will remain in your Deleted Items folder until you decide to empty it. Right click the folder, or select Edit, Empty Deleted Items folder.

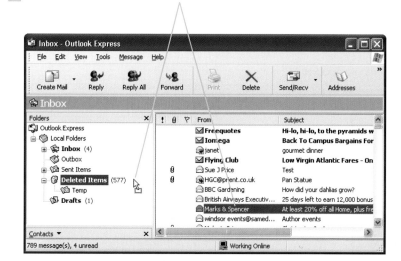

Select Tools, Options, and click the Maintenance tab to see ways to manage message storage.

3 To delete several messages at once: select the first item, then hold down Ctrl and select the others. For a block of files, select the first item, then hold down the Shift and click on the last. Press delete.

You cannot drag and drop items into the Outbox. You will get a No Entry symbol as you pass over the folder.

4 The messages arrive and are stored in date order. Click Received in the heading to reverse the order and view the oldest messages. Click From to view them grouped by sender.

5 You can create your own folders to organise your e-mail. Select the main folder, right click and select New Folder from the menu. Name the folder, then drag and drop messages into it.

Print your e-mail

You will need to provide a print of your Inbox and of your file working (storage) area.

Use the method described and illustrated in Unit 1 to create a screen print and annotate it. See page 53.

New CLAiT requires you to provide printed copies of all the e-mail you have sent and received. Make sure that Outlook Express is set up to save a copy of all the e-mail you send into the Sent folder (see page 219).

To print messages in the Inbox or the Sent folder:

1   Open the message. Then select File, Print, or click the printer button.

2   The Print dialog box opens, and allows you to select a page range, and number of copies. If you have more than one printer defined you can also select the printer. Click Print to action the request.

You can print a message without opening it. Select it from the folder and click the Print button.

To print the attachment, save it to disk, and use the appropriate software to view and print it.

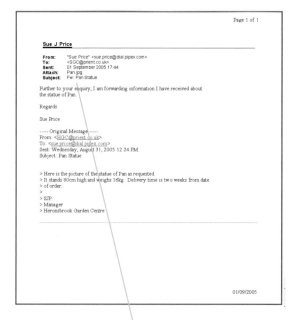

Outlook Express should automatically include all the required details in the header, but do check the printout to make sure.

3   The printed e-mail for a reply or forward must show Re: or Fw: and the original subject heading. The address on a reply must be the same as that on the original message. If the message had an attachment, that also must show in the heading when forwarding.

The World Wide Web

Internet Explorer is the web browser supplied by Microsoft. It can be started from the Start menu, or from the Quick Launch bar.

The Home Page

The first screen that you will see is known as the Home page. As Internet Explorer is a Microsoft product, the standard is to open with the Microsoft Home page. You will see the MSN address in the address bar. The page presents you with information, news, advertisements etc., and a series of links to other pages.

Notice also the scroll bars at the side of the page. The full Home page is not displayed.

You can select any web page for your home page, or none at all. Select Tools, Internet Options, and view the alternatives.

URLs or web addresses are complex and must be typed exactly as specified. However, once you start using the Internet you will find that you seldom need to type them yourself. You can use the hyperlinks provided, or use the Favorites and History features provided with Internet Explorer.

Internet Explorer Toolbar   Hotmail e-mail   Chat rooms   Search

Status bar displaying address of selected link   News   Links to topics

Do not rely on Internet Explorer to complete Internet addresses for you, as this facility must be disabled during the exam.

You can navigate the Internet by typing any address into the address bar. Then click on Go. This is sometimes the most efficient way to use the Internet. Click the down arrow on the Address bar to select sites previously visited. Alternatively, you can use the hypertext links that are found on most pages. Use the toolbar with its Back, Forward etc. buttons for navigating whilst you are surfing.

The Links

A link, or more correctly a hypertext link, is a pointer to the address of either another part of the same page, another page on the same site or another site altogether. To recognise a link, pass the mouse pointer over the screen. It changes to a hand when on a link. A link may also be indicated by underlined text. A link on a web page is created by using a Uniform Resource Locator (URL).

The URL

This is the address of a web site. It takes the following form:

If the new page has many images, it may take a long time to load. Watch the progression on the status bar to make sure it is still loading the information.

http://www.msn.co.uk/default.asp

access mechanism   server   page

Click on the link and you will be taken to that address. The status bar shows the page opening and the progress.

The Internet Explorer Toolbar

There are two meanings of Home page. One you select for your Home page when you open Internet Explorer, the other is a site Home page. When you click the Home button you return to your starting Home page.

Use Stop (loading) if you change your mind after selecting a link.

Back to the previous page   Stop loading   Home   MSN search   History

Forward to next page   Refresh current page   Index of favourite sites   Music, radio and video

Search engines

There is so much information on the Internet that it is now essential to know how to use a search engine, and it is useful to become familiar with more than one as they frequently produce different results.

Using the toolbar Search button will override any other Search engine you may have open.

MSN Searches

If you use Internet Explorer as your browser, the Search button on the toolbar will automatically invoke the MSN search engine.

Click the Search button to open the Search panel.

Type in the search topic and click on Go.

The down arrow next to the Back button allows you to select which page to revisit.

Searching on 'Roses' with MSN Search returned over 15 million results within 0.15 seconds.

To return to the Search results page, select the Back button.

Pruning Roses ... HYBRID TEA, FLORIBUNDA AND SHRUB ROSES Prune your new roses around March - April...

2 The results of the search will show in both the Search panel and the main window which is used to Preview results pages.

3 To view the next and subsequent results pages, scroll to the bottom of the Search panel and click Next.

4 When you find a site that interests, click on the link, indicated by the mouse pointer changing to a hand.

Searching on 'Roses' with Google.com returned 10.5 million results. Using Google.co.uk reduced the results to 995,000.

Google searches

Google (http://www.google.com) has become a popular search engine, using a very clear and simple format. You can search for web pages, images, discussion groups, or news, and you can limit searches to the UK right from the start.

Google has an 'I'm Feeling Lucky' option to take you, hopefully, directly to the right site.

Even so, the results of a search will still return so many hits that it becomes essential to learn some of the more advanced tricks and techniques to refine and limit your search.

For New CLAiT you must provide a printout with the required information, not just a search engine list of sites.

Click the Advanced Search option on the right, and complete as many of the fields as possible. Click the Google Search button.

When looking for news reports or dated information, use the option to limit the search to web pages updated and specify a time period.

This time the search returned 972 hits, the first few of which were particularly appropriate.

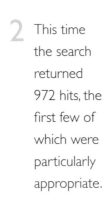

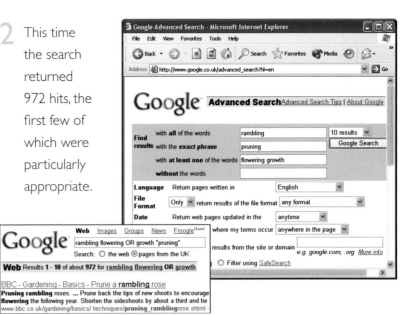

Many web sites will also have links to other web sites of similar content or interest.

Local Search engines

Most web sites consist of several web pages. They will have their own Home page, navigation facility and often a search engine as well. The search engine works within the site, and all resulting links will be to pages within the site.

This site offers its own navigation facility. Click any tab, for example Books or Music, to go directly to that category of items for sale.

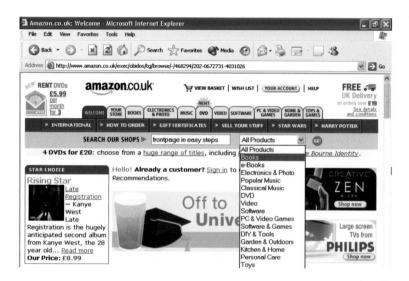

1. This web site has a search facility on the main Home page. Type in the topic of interest, limit the search to books and click Go.

Some web sites allow you to set up lists of items of interest, preferences, or will maintain a history of your visits and searches.

2. The required book should appear at the top of the list.

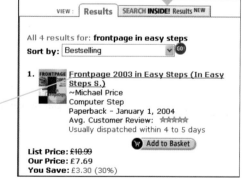

3. Click the underlined title to follow the link to see a larger photo of the cover and read more about the book and its contents.

4. To purchase the book click the link to Add to Basket.

Save images and text

This toolbar will only appear if the image size is 200x200 pixels or more, and if you have Internet Explorer v6 or later.

Save the image · e-mail · Image toolbar

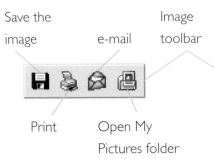

Print · Open My Pictures folder

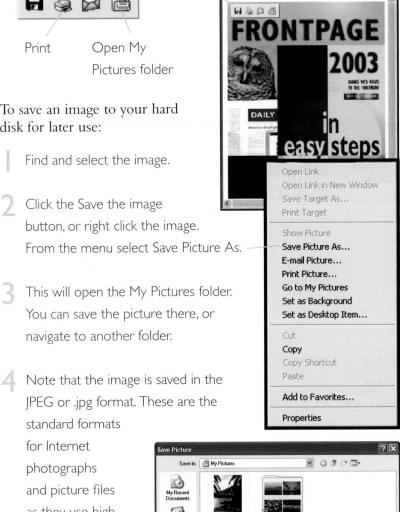

To save an image to your hard disk for later use:

1. Find and select the image.

2. Click the Save the image button, or right click the image. From the menu select Save Picture As.

For New CLAiT you must find the required image and save it to your hard disk so that you can then attach it to an e-mail. It is not sufficient to use the menu option to e-mail the picture.

3. This will open the My Pictures folder. You can save the picture there, or navigate to another folder.

4. Note that the image is saved in the JPEG or .jpg format. These are the standard formats for Internet photographs and picture files as they use high compression.

.gif files are used for icons and small images.

5. Click on Save, making a note of the file name.

Web pages can be constructed in different ways and a neat A4 printout is not guaranteed. Check using Print Preview to see how a web page will print and how many pages it may take.

You can learn more about web page construction in Unit 7. See page 199.

If you just want to save and view items from a web page, Word is a good application to use. It works well with a combination of text and graphics and is also able to create and work with .htm and .html files – the format for web pages.

You must be very careful not to infringe copyright. If in any doubt, contact the Web Master for the site.

The method you use to save text from a web page will depend on how much text you wish to copy, and your purpose in copying.

1 For a small amount of text, to be used in Word or a text application, use the normal copy and paste facility. Select the text with the mouse or cursor, right click and choose Copy from the Context menu. Open Word or another text application and paste. The pasted text is normal unformatted text.

2 For the whole contents of the web page, text and images, you can use Edit, Select all or Ctrl+A and copy. Open Word and select paste. The pasted items may carry certain attributes with them, and the result in Word may be different than you'd expect. The objects may be encased in frames or need to be realigned on the page. You then have the choice to save the document as a standard .doc file, or as an .htm or .html.

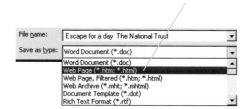

3 Unlike Word, Internet Explorer is specifically designed to work with web pages, and offers to Edit with Microsoft FrontPage. Using this, you could capture objects from web pages and use them for your own purposes. When you save the file, .htm and .html are the default, or you can choose a text file.

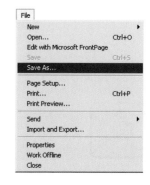

Manage web addresses

The History button lists web sites visited over a period of time. You can use web addresses from the list. Open and close History as for Favorites.

Internet Explorer provides the Favorites function to allow you to store web addresses that you wish to use again.

1   Make sure that you are viewing the page that you wish to bookmark or add to your favorites list. Select Favorites from the menu.

2   Click Add to Favorites. The Add Favorite dialog box picks up the title of the site and its Internet address. To help with the organisation, it allows you to collect related links together in folders of favorites.

You can also right click a web page and select Add to Favorites from there.

3   To use an existing folder, select "Create in" and the list of folders expands for you to select. For a new topic, select New Folder. Type in the folder name and then click OK.

You don't have to organise your Favorites into folders, but over a period of time it makes sense.

4   To view the list of Favorites, select the Favorites button on the toolbar. The list of your bookmarked or saved addresses will appear in a separate pane on the left of the screen. Click a folder to open it and select from the list. Close the folder using the Close button (X) on the Favorites pane to return to the full web page screen.

Both the Favorites and History buttons are toggles – click once to open, click again to close.

Printing web pages

Web pages do not necessarily conform to screen or paper dimensions and screen and printer resolutions also differ. Much of the time you can only see a portion of the web page, the scroll bars allow you to see the rest. It is always worth previewing the printed output first to ascertain just how many pages you will take, and whether it will look the way you expect.

I   With your required web page on the screen, select File, Print Preview. The toolbar shows Page 1 of 1, and the magnification.

Select Setup and change the paper size to A4 if necessary.

If the text does truncate, check to make sure that the page has the required information.

2   Notice how the titles have been truncated on the right. Also, the original text background was green, but is rendered as white when printed.

You can print a table of links, useful if you are doing research and need to keep track of sites visited.

3   Some web pages are composed of 'frames' which can be printed together, as on the screen, or individually.

Unit 8 exercise

You are allowed two and a half hours to complete this assignment.

Scenario

You work as an assistant to the manager at Surprise Gardens.

Task 1

You have been sent an e-mail message.

See page 254 for information on how to receive an initial e-mail message with an attachment. The message will come from the Heronsbrook manager at HGC@prient.co.uk

1. Open your mailbox and read the message entitled Pan Statue.
2. Save the attachment Pan.jpg outside the mailbox in your work area.
3. Scan the attachment Pan.jpg for viruses. Make a note of the name of the virus scanning software.
4. Add the sender's e-mail address to your address book.
5. Print a copy of the address book entry.
6. Your manager is interested in buying the statue. Forward the message Pan Statue and its attachment to your manager at SGC@prient.co.uk, adding the following text:

    Further to your enquiry, I am forwarding information I have received about the statue of Pan.

7. Add your name and exam centre number to the end of your message.
8. Check your message for errors and forward the e-mail message including the attachment. Make sure that your system keeps a copy of the outgoing message.

Task 2

You should acknowledge receipt of the original e-mail.

1. Prepare a reply to the Heronsbrook Manager with the following message:

    Thank you for the information about the Pan statue. I will contact you again once a decision has been made.

2. Add your name and exam centre number to the end of your message.
3. Check your message for errors and send the e-mail message. Make sure that your system keeps a copy of the outgoing message.

You need to manage your mailbox to reduce storage demands.

4. Delete the message Pan Statue.

5. Produce a printout of the contents of your Inbox. A screen print is acceptable.

6. Add your name and Centre number to the print.

Task 3

Your manager will give a talk on the National Trust and has asked you to find information about local National Trust activities.

1. Use a web-based search engine to search for web pages that contain information about the National Trust. Follow links to find specific information about activities in your area.

Sample picture

2. Bookmark the page and print one copy.

Your manager has suggested that you might find it helpful in your work if you had some computer reference books to hand.

3. Access the Amazon web site at www.amazon.co.uk.

4. Click the Books link and use the local search facility to find books on FrontPage.

5. Follow the link to FrontPage in easy steps and bookmark the page.

6. Follow the link to see a larger photo.

7. Save the book front cover as an image named Frontpage.jpg into your work area.

8. Print one copy of the cover of the FrontPage book.

9. Produce a screen print of your Favorites folder showing the two bookmarked pages.

Task 4

1. Prepare an e-mail to send to your manager at SGC@prient.co.uk.

2. Give the message the subject heading: Reference Books

Use the following message:

Here is the front cover of one of the reference books I would find very useful. Please let me know if I am able to order it.

3. Locate and attach the file Frontpage.jpg.

4. Add your name and exam centre number to the end of your message.

5. Send a copy (Cc:) of the message to the Heronsbrook Manager, using the e-mail address from your Address book.

6. Check your message for errors and send the e-mail message including the attachment. Make sure that your system keeps a copy of the outgoing message.

7   Take a screen print of your working area, making sure that the files Pan.jpg and Frontpage.jpg are visible.

8. Locate copies of the messages you have sent and print a copy of each message. There should be three prints:

    the forwarded message to your manager

    the reply to the Heronsbrook manager

    the new message Reference Books sent to your manager

9. Make sure header details (To, From, Date, Subject) are shown. Make sure attachment details are shown where appropriate.

You should have the following prints:

    a copy of the Address Book entry

    a printout of the contents of your Inbox

    a printout of National Trust activities in your area

    a printout of the cover of the FrontPage book

    a screen print of your Favorites folder

    a screen print of your work area

    printouts of the three e-mail messages

IC³, Webwise and Downloads

This section introduces the units that are supported by external tests – the three IC³ units, and the BBC's Webwise Course, an alternative route for Unit Eight. It also explains how to visit the In Easy Steps web site and download all the files that you need to make full use of the exercises in this book.

Covers

The IC³ Exams | 246

IC³ Exam Demo | 247

IC³ Exam Objectives | 248

BBC Webwise | 251

Download files | 253

Where next? | 255

Units Nine, Ten, Eleven

The IC³ Exams

IC³ stands for Internet and Computing Core Certification and is exam based certification managed by Certiport. There are three exams, each of which equates to a New CLAiT 2006 unit:

The assessment for each IC³ unit takes the form of an on-line test using Certiport Software. It is composed of both practical tasks and multiple choice items. The whole test takes approximately 45 minutes to complete.

- Computing Fundamentals   Unit 9
- Key Applications   Unit 10
- Living Online   Unit 11

You may choose one or more of these as your optional units for the New CLAiT certificate or diploma. To achieve IC³ certification you would need to take and pass all three IC³ exams.

There are two versions of each of these exams: IC³ 2003 Standard and IC³ 2005 Standard. The newer standard incorporates advances in technology such as interactive books, PDAs and cell phones, and current issues such as the latest Internet security threats. However, either standard is currently acceptable for the purposes of New CLAiT 2006.

The IC³ units may be provided by awarding bodies other than OCR centres. However, the only way these units can contribute to achieving the NQF-accredited New CLAiT 2006 qualification is if they have been achieved through an OCR centre as part of the OCR CLAiT Suite.

The main objectives for each of these exams (IC³ 2005 Standard) are listed on pages 248-250. For more information on IC³, including details of courseware, books and practice exams, visit the Certiport web site at http://www.certiport.com.

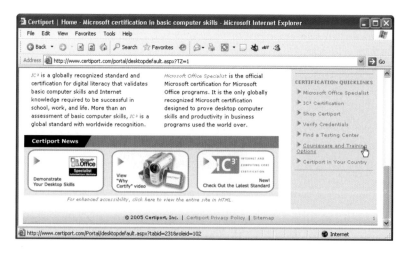

There is also a UK Certiport web site at http://www.certiport.co.uk which may be useful for regional information such as testing centres and local resources, or for special promotions in the UK.

IC³ Exam Demo

There is a useful presentation with sample exam questions available for download from www.certiport.com, but it is rather well buried.

1 Select IC³ Certification from the Quicklinks listed on the right hand side.

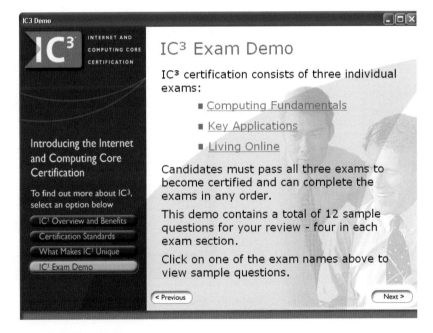

CERTIFICATION QUICKLINKS
▶ Microsoft Office Specialist
▶ IC³ Certification
▶ Shop Certiport

2 From the next web page, select the IC³ Exam Demo Quicklink.

QUICKLINKS
▶ IC³ Exam Demo
▶ Certiport Career Planner
▶ Find a Testing Center

3 Click the IC³ Exam Demonstration arrow, to display the details for this facility.

IC³
EXAM DEMONSTRATION

4 Click on the link to Download Questions and Presentation, to obtain this 4Mb file.

Download Questions and Presentation

5 Run the downloaded ic3Overview.exe to install the presentation, which will be added to All Programs list in the Start menu.

With the performance-based questions, you carry out the instructions as if you were using the actual software.

The presentation gives an overview of IC³ and provides four sample questions for each exam, a mix of knowledge-based (multiple choice) and performance-based (practical) questions.

IC³ Exam Objectives

The exam objectives for IC³ may be updated periodically, but you will always find the latest version at the Certiport web site. The objectives as specified for the IC³ 2005 standard are as follows:

IC³ Computing Fundamentals
Computer Hardware:

Identify types of computers, how they process information and how individual computers interact with other computing systems and devices.

Identify the function of computer hardware components.

Identify the factors that go into an individual or organisational decision on how to purchase computer equipment.

Identify how to maintain computer equipment and solve common problems relating to computer hardware.

Computer Software:

Identify how software and hardware work together to perform computing tasks and how software is developed and upgraded.

Identify different types of software, general concepts relating to software categories, and the tasks to which each type of software is most suited or not suited.

Identify fundamental concepts relating to database applications.

This is a sample knowledge-based question for the Computing Fundamentals exam, taken from the Certiport IC3 Exam Demo. Drag the appropriate answers to the boxes next to the related statements.

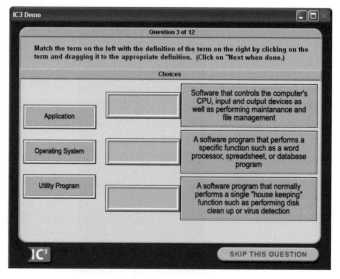

Using an Operating System:

Identify what an operating system is and how it works, and solve common problems related to operating systems.

Manipulate and control the Windows desktop, files and disks.

Identify how to change system settings, install and remove software.

IC³ Key Applications
Common Program Functions:

> Be able to start and exit a Windows application and utilize sources of on-line help.
> Identify common on-screen elements of Windows applications, change application settings and manage files within an application.
> Perform common editing and formatting functions.
> Perform common printing functions.

Word Processing Functions:

> Be able to format text and documents including the ability to use automatic formatting tools.
> Be able to insert, edit and format tables in a document.

Spreadsheet Functions:

> Be able to modify worksheet data and structure and format data in a worksheet.
> Be able to sort data, manipulate data using formulas and functions and add and modify charts in a worksheet.

This is a sample knowledge-based question for the Key Applications exam, taken from the Certiport IC3 Exam Demo. You select the answer from the choices provided.

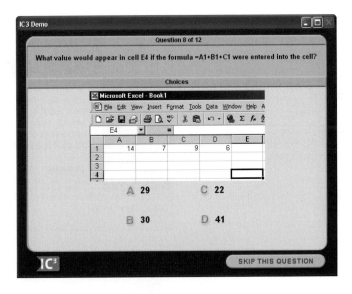

Presentation Software:

> Be able to create and format simple presentations.
>
> NB: This means being able to identify effective design principles for simple presentations, manage slides (create, insert, delete, duplicate), add information, change view, and layout, modify background and assign transitions.

IC³ Living Online

Networks and the Internet:

Identify network fundamentals and the benefits and risks of network computing.

Identify the relationship between computer networks, other communications networks (like the telephone network) and the Internet.

There are no general rules for the combination of optional units, with the exception of Unit 8 (see page 213) and Unit 11 where only one of these units can be claimed towards either of the full Certificate or the full Diploma.

Electronic Mail:

Identify how electronic mail works.

Identify how to use an electronic mail application.

Identify the appropriate use of e-mail and e-mail related "netiquette".

Using the Internet:

Identify different types of information sources on the Internet.

Be able to use a Web browsing application.

Be able to search the Internet for information.

This is a sample performance-based question for the Living Online exam, taken from the Certiport IC3 Exam Demo. You answer it by clicking the History button, just as you would in Internet Explorer.

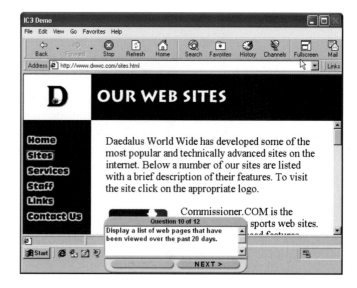

The Impact of Computing and the Internet on Society:

Identify how computers are used in different areas of work, school, and home.

Identify the risks of using computer hardware and software.

Identify how to use the Internet safely, legally, and responsibly.

NB: Risks of computing include loss of autonomy, potential loss of privacy and security, potential of network-wide systems failure and vulnerability to a network virus attack.

BBC Webwise

The BBC Webwise Course provides an alternative way to achieve New CLAiT Unit 8 - Online Communications.

BBC Becoming Webwise, which formed unit 11 in the original New CLAiT, has been revised and renamed as the Webwise Course. Anyone who has successfully completed this can claim it as evidence of achievement towards New CLAiT 2006 Level 1 Unit 8, Online Communication.

You'll find the starting point to the Webwise course at the BBC's Web site at www.bbc.co.uk/webwise/course.

You cannot count the Webwise course towards the New CLAiT qualification, if you have already included Unit 8, or Unit 11 – Living Online (see page 250). You should still consider the Webwise course as a tutorial as it provides useful information and is very worthwhile.

The Webwise Course is a ten hour, online internet course which teaches the basics of using the internet. It uses a guided discovery learning approach where you try and guess the best way to do things and have a go when you don't know the answer. The individual units contain interactive guides, with a quiz following each guide. There's also an online mission designed to use new skills and a Weakest Link quiz for each unit.

The course has ten units, each lasting one hour and it is intended for beginners working at Level 1 (though some of the content relates to level 2 objectives).

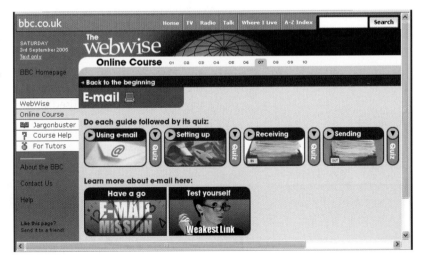

The course also includes the Jargonbuster (a simple glossary of terms), the Help section, and some online computer games. You can print out a progress chart to keep a manual record of which guides, quizzes and extra activities you have completed.

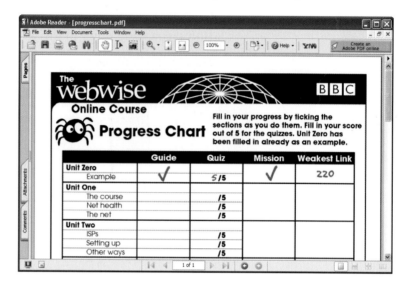

The Webwise course can be used towards a number of qualifications, including LCCIEB Practical Computing, NCFE Certificate in Telematics (Basic), SQA Internet Basics and City and Guilds 7261 Information Technology, as well as OCR New CLAiT Level 1. You must register and take the examination at an authorised centre to receive accreditation.

You can complete the course at home (if you have Internet access) or at one of the Webwise partner learning centres. After you've finished the course material, you'll be able to take a one hour assessment that leads to a qualification. You take the assessment online at a supervised centre. It consists of twelve multiple-choice questions and three short practical tasks (browsing, searching, e-mail). To pass, you must get at least seven out of twelve multiple choice questions right and successfully complete all three tasks.

Computer Tutor

BBC Webwise also offers an introductory course for beginners who don't know how to use a keyboard, mouse or computer screen. It is set in Game Show World, a theme park about TV game shows, and learners visit each studio where they pick up a new computer skill then practise that skill in a game show.

The course takes two to three hours to complete, but can be tackled in short sessions, using the Return Visitor button on subsequent visits.

Download files

The exercises for each unit require data files to get you started. On a New CLAiT course, these might be provided for you, in folders specified by your tutor. If you are using this book for self study, you can download a set of exercise files from the In Easy Steps web site: http://www.ineasysteps.com/resources/downloads/

The folders include the files needed for the exercises described at the end of each unit. See page 55 for an example. Please note that only files that are required for the exercises are included in the download, not every file used for illustration.

1 Visit **http://www.ineasysteps.com/resources/downloads/** and under the Exercises heading locate the New CLAiT 2006 entry.

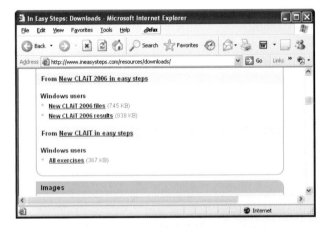

There are two download links for this book. The first is for the data files, and the second is for the results files (see page 254).

2 Select the "New CLAiT 2006 files" link and click Save to download the self-extracting file NewCLAIT2006_files.exe.

3 Choose a location, for example C:\Downloads, to store the files and folders on your hard disk, then click the Save button.

4 Double click the downloaded file to create the files and folders for the New CLAiT 2006 exercises.

The folder named NC2006data, will contain a subfolder for each of the units. There's also an NC2006photos folder for use in Unit 6 (Computer Art).

The third folder NC2006results, is downloaded separately, and contains sample prints for each of the units, in .pdf format.

5 By default, the folders and files are created in C:\, but you can specify any drive or folder. Click Unzip to extract the files and folders, then click OK, Close.

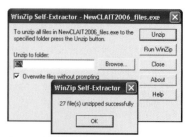

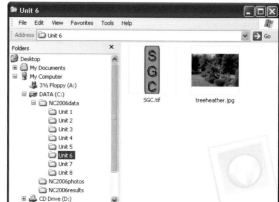

To view the eight .pdf files, with the expected prints for each unit, download the free Adobe Reader from the web site www.Adobe.com/

6 Select the "New CLAiT 2006 results" link to download the file NewCLAiT2006_results.exe and run this to obtain the .pdf files.

Electronic Communications

Unit 8 requires no data files, but it does need an initial email.

Visit http://newclait2006.prient.co.uk/ and enter your e-mail ID, to request the email message and attachment needed.

Submitting your email ID at this web page automatically generates an email with an attachment, as required for the unit 8 exercise.

Note that this web page also includes a link to the In Easy Steps download site.

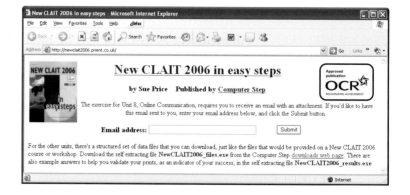

Where next?

Certification is also available for single units, at all levels, and you could take individual units to prepare yourself for the next stage.

New CLAiT 2006

In order to achieve a certificate qualification, you are required to achieve three units, the mandatory Unit 1, plus two additional optional units. When you have completed this, you could carry on to achieve a diploma qualification, by passing a further two of the optional units.

CLAiT Plus 2006

As New CLAiT is the OCR Level 1 Certificate for IT Users, the next obvious step for those who are successful is to take CLAiT Plus, the Level 2 Certificate for IT Users. This certificate follows the general approach set at Level 1. You are again required to take a mandatory Unit 1 plus two optional units for a certificate, or four optional units for a diploma. The units offered are:

Unit 1   Integrated e-document production

Unit 2   Manipulating spreadsheets and graphs

Unit 3   Creating and using a Database

Unit 4   E-publication design

Unit 5   Design an e-presentation

Unit 6   E-image manipulation

Unit 7   Website creation

Unit 8   Electronic communication

Assessment is by means of an OCR-set practical assignment with a notional duration of 3 hours. The assignment is set in a realistic scenario and is designed to allow you to use your knowledge and understanding to demonstrate skill in each assessment objective in a logical and realistic way.

Alternatively, assessment may be means of a scenario devised locally by the centre, or by you, the candidate. There are no time restrictions on the number of hours you may take to achieve the assessment, this is left to the centres. A guide could be 10 – 15 hours.

When you have achieved the certificate CLAiT Level 2, you may be advised to consider further individual certificates or the diploma option within the CLAiT Plus syllabus before progressing onto Level 3.

CLAiT Advanced 2006

CLAiT Advanced is the OCR Level 3 Certificate for IT Users, which offers a total of seven units, the first of which is mandatory. As at the other levels, you are required to take the mandatory Unit 1 plus two optional units for a certificate, or four optional units for a diploma. The units offered are:

Unit 1   Creating an IT solution

Unit 2   Analysing spreadsheets and graphs

Unit 3   Relational databases

Unit 4   E-publication production

Unit 5   Professional e-presentation

Unit 6   E-image production

Unit 7   Website authoring

All units are assessed by means of a scenario and an associated OCR evidence checklist. Centres may use the OCR devised scenarios, alternatively the centre or the candidate may wish to develop scenarios for use with the OCR Evidence Checklist. There is no time limit for the assignment and all work must be completed under supervised conditions.

Microsoft Office Specialist

These tests may be claimed as evidence of achievement towards particular CLAiT units:

MOS Unit	CLAiT Plus Unit
Word Core	1 - Integrated e-Document Production
Excel Core	2 - Manipulating Spreadsheets and Graphs
Access Core	3 - Creating and Using a Database
PowerPoint Core	5 - Design an e-Presentation
Outlook Core	8 - Electronic Communication

	CLAiT Advanced Unit
Word Expert	1 - Creating an IT Solution
Excel Expert	2 - Analysing Spreadsheets and Graphs

Index

A

Address Book 221, 222, 229
Adobe software 169
ADSL 215
Alignment 40, 137, 201
Annotate photograph 181
Antialias 166, 167
Assessment 246, 252, 255
Attachment 230
Automatic filename 44, 79
AutoShapes
    Desktop publishing 128, 140
    PowerPoint 157
AutoSum 69
Autotext 44, 79, 150
Average function 70

B

Backspace 31
Bar/column chart 88
Bcc 226
Bitmap images 166
Borders and shading 77
Border art 141
Broadband 215
Browser 190, 191, 215
Bullets and numbering 48
Button 17

C

Cancel print 52
Capitalisation 30

Cc: 226
Cell reference 60
Certificate 255
Certiport 246
Change column widths 106
Change scale 88, 92
Chart Options 90
Chart toolbar 91
CLAiT Advanced 2006 256
CLAiT Plus 2006 255
CLAiT units 12, 255
Clipboard 42
Close 36
Close button 17, 36
Close database 119
Close Program window 54
Columns 62
Column gutter 133
Composite print 143
Computer art
    Adobe software 169
    Bitmaps 166
    Canvas 171
    Corel software 168
    Creating artwork 166
    File format 166
    Insert images 172, 173
    Print 178, 180, 183
    Raster images 166
    Vector images 167
    Visio 168
Computer hardware 10, 15
    Keyboard 11, 13, 28
    Monitor 10, 13, 14
    Mouse 11, 13
    Systems unit 10, 14
Computer software 12
    Office XP 12
        Access 12
        Excel 59, 60
        FrontPage 12, 190
        Outlook 214
        Outlook Express 214
        PowerPoint 148
        Publisher 126
        Visio 168
        Word 25, 126
    Operating system 12, 15
        Internet Explorer 15
Computer Tutor 252
Computing Fundamentals 248

Connected frames 133
Copying files 22
Copy image 178, 179
Copy text 41
Corel software 168
Course requirements 253, 255
Create, Manage and Integrate Files
    Bullets and numbering 48
    Folder commands 21
    Footers 44
    Headers 44
    Identify files 24
    Manage files 22
    Print folder contents 53
    Tabs 47
    View folders 18
Create an e-Presentation 147
Create canvas 171
Creating Spreadsheets and Graphs 59
Crop 174
Cut and Paste 65

D

Database 102
    Add records 107
    Amend records 107
    Change column widths 106
    Close 119
    Create 103
    Create query 112
    Create table 120
    Data types 105, 121
    Delete records 107
    Design 109, 120
    Edit table 107
    Excel facilities 66
    Filters 110
    Filter by form 110
    Filter by selection 110
    Find and replace 108
    Forms 104
    Matching 111
    Microsoft Access 102
    Microsoft Excel 102
    Pages 104
    Printing queries 114, 115
    Printing tables 114, 115
    Queries 104, 111
    Reports 104
    Run query 113
    Save query 113

Sort 109
Start Access 103
Tables 104, 105
Table tools 109, 110
Undo 107
Window 104
Database Manipulation 101
Data types 24, 35, 105, 121, 166
Default printer 51
Delete text 31
Deleting files 23
Desktop publishing 126
    Active frame 131
    Advanced print settings 143
    AutoShapes 128, 140
    Blank publications 127, 128
    Borders 141
    Columns 132, 133
    Column gutter 133
    Column widths 133
    Composite print 143
    Connected frames 133
    Create text box link 133
    Delete frame 132
    Design checker 132, 142
    Design wizard 126, 127
    Drawing tools 140
    Fonts 136
    Font schemes 136
    Font sizes 136
    Frames 131
    Image management 139
    Import image 138
    Import text 134, 135
    Layout guides 129, 142
    Line spacing 142
    Link indicator 133
    Margin guides 129, 131
    Menu bar 128
    Mirrored guides 129
    Objects toolbar 128
    Overflow indicator 133, 134, 135
    Page layout 129
    Picture frame 131
    Pitcher 133
    Printing 143
    Publications by Design 127
    Publication Gallery 127, 130
    Publisher window 128
    Rotation handle 139
    Save as Publisher file 130
    Save as template 130
    Selection handles 131, 139
    Start Publisher 127
    Templates 130
    Text alignment 137
    Text box 131
    Text box layout 132

Tolerance 142
Word vs Publisher 126
Wrapping style 139
Digital photographs 180
Storage card 180
Diploma 255
Document management
Headers and Footers 78
Document standards 30
Document views 27
Drawing tools
Desktop publishing 140
Drive letter 10
DTP 126

E

e-Document Production 9
e-Image Creation 165
E-mail 214
e-Presentation 147
e-Publication Creation 125
Editing text 31
Electronic communication
Connection 215
E-mail 213, 214
Address book 221
Attachments 230
Create e-mail 225
Folders 219, 231
Forward 227, 229
Inbox 219, 220
Outbox 219
Print 232
Send/Receive, 219, 227, 228
Send Later 227
Internet 213, 215, 233
Home Page 233
Images 238
Links 234, 240
Printing 241
Search engines 235, 237
Text 239
Receive attachments 223
Exercises
Download files 253
Results 254
Unit 1 55
Unit 2 97
Unit 3 122
Unit 4 144
Unit 5 162

Unit 6 185
Unit 7 210
Unit 8 242
Existing file 37

F

File formats 24, 25, 134, 166
File Management 9, 22, 65
File Transfer Protocol 209
Fill tool 72
Filters 110
Filter by form 110
Filter by selection 110
Find and replace 43, 108
Firewall 216
Fit to page 80
Flip image 139, 179
Folders
Create 21
Explore 18
Navigate 20
Rename 21
Fonts 136
Format Painter 137, 200
Format text 39
Formulae 67
Copying 73
Printing 81
Recalculate 74
Formula bar 60, 67
Freeze Panes 61
FrontPage Server Extensions 209
Functions 68
Arguments 71
AutoSum 69, 70
Average 70
Max and Min 71
Sum 69
Function key 11

G

Grammar checking 33
Graphs and charts
Axis labels 88, 90

Chart data 83
Chart objects 91
Chart title 90
Chart toolbar 91
Chart types 82
   Bar chart 82, 88
   Column charts 82, 88
   Line graph 82, 89
   Pie chart 82, 84, 95
Chart wizard 84, 88, 93
Data labels 86
Editing charts 90
Embedded object 87
Legend 86, 91, 93
Parts of a chart 83
Printing charts 96
Scales 92
Series 85, 94, 95
Greyscale 143
Grid lines 46, 60, 79
Gutter 133

Headers and footers 44, 78, 96, 118
Header row 66
Help 11
History 20
Hourglass symbol 14
House style
   Desktop publishing 127
   Presentation graphics 150
   Web pages 201
HTML 190
HTML Editors 190
HTML file format 191
Hypertext Transfer Protocol 209

IC³ 246
IC³ Exam Demo 247
IC³ Exam Objectives 248
Icons 15, 16
Image resolution 171, 182
Indents 47, 137

Insert image 172, 173
Internet 215, 233
   connection 215
Internet Explorer 191
Internet Service Provider (ISP) 191, 209, 214

Jargonbuster 252
Jasc software 168
Justify text 32, 40, 146

Keyboard 11, 13, 28
   Select text 38
Key Applications 249

Layers palette 179
Ledger sheet 60
Line graph 89
Line spacing 40, 142
Links 234
Living Online 250
Log on 54
Long integer 121

Magnification 172
Mandatory unit 9, 255
Margins 29, 30, 129

Menu bar 17, 128
Microsoft Office Specialist 256
Microsoft Word 26
Mirror guides 129
Mirror image 179
Monitor 10, 13, 14
   Resolution 10
Mouse 11, 13
Move text 41
Moving files 23
My Computer 15, 19
My Documents 15

N

Navigate folders 20
Netscape 191, 215
New Folder 21
Notepad 25
Notification Area 51
Numbering 48

O

Object selection 178
Office XP 12
Online Communication 213
Open file 37
Opera 215
Operating system 12, 15
Operators 67
Outlook 214
Outlook Express 214
   Folders 219
   Off-line 218
   Start 218

P

Page layout 29, 129

Page views 27
Paint Shop Pro 168, 170
   Layers palette 179
   Preset shape 176
   Raster layer 173, 179
   Vector layer 175, 176
   Vector text 177
Paint Shop Pro Studio 170
Password 14
Pause print 52
Pie chart 84
Pie chart segments 95
Pixelated 166
Popup blocker 216
POST 14
Power off 54
Presentation graphics 148
   Arranging slides 158
   Bulleted text 155
   Bullets 151
   Bullet levels 151, 155
   Clip art 149
   Design templates. 149
   Handouts 159
   New presentation 149
   Numbering 151
   Outline view 158
   PowerPoint 148
   Printing 159
   Selection handles 153
   Slide 148
   Slide layout 149, 154
   Slide master 150, 151, 152, 154
      Insert image 153
      Text areas 152
   Slide Show 161
      Animation scheme 161
      Transition effects 161
   Slide sorter view 158
   Task pane 148
   Text box 150, 151
   Text levels 151
   Text tools 156, 157
      Autofit 156
      Find 156
      Replace 156
      Spell checker 156
   Title master 154
   WordArt 149
Preset shape 176
Printer 51
Printing 52
   Charts 96
   Desktop publishing 143
   E-mail 232
   Formulae 81
   Internet 241
   Local 51

Network 51
Pause 52
Presentation graphics 159
Print document 50
Print preview 49
Properties 51
Queries 114, 115
Spool 52
Spreadsheets 80
Tables 114, 115
Print folder contents 53
Print preview 49, 81
Print screen 53
Progress chart 252
Publisher desktop 126

Q

Queries
    Create 112
    Criteria 111
    Design 111, 113
    Printing 114
    Run 113
Quick Launch bar 15, 16, 218

R

Range 61
    Fill tool 72
Raster images 166
Raster layer 173, 179
Receive attachments 223
Recycle bin 15
Redo 32
Repetitive strain injury 13
Reports 115
Resolution
    Image 171, 172, 182
    Screen 10
Restart 54
Ruler 27, 29, 45, 49

S

Sans serif fonts 136
Save 34, 36
Save As 35
Save as template 130
Scale 88, 92, 167
Scan Disk program 54
Screentips 28
Screen print 53
Scroll bar 17
Search engines 235, 237
Selecting cells 61
Select text 38
Send/Receive, 219
Serif fonts 136
Show/hide 40
Shutdown 54
Smart Tag 42, 64
Sort
    Database 109
    Report 115
    Spreadsheet 66
Spacebar 11
Spell checking 25, 33, 126, 152, 156
Spreadsheet 59, 60
    Absolute reference 73
    Alignment 64
    Borders and shading 77
    Cell reference 60, 67
    Columns 62, 63, 64
    Create 62
    Delete 64, 65
    Fill tool 72
    Format cells 75
    Formulae 67
    Freeze panes 61
    Functions 68
    Grid 60
    Hide columns 64
    Insert column 74
    Layout 63
    Move 65
    Numeric format 75
    Print 80
    Print headings and gridlines 79
    Range 61, 68, 70
    Relative reference 73
    Selecting cells 61
    Sort 66
    Text format 76
    Toolbars 60
    Undo 64
    Window 60

Standard window 17
Stand By mode 54
Start button 15, 54
Start menu 16
Start menu. 127
Status bar 17, 26
Stroke and Fill 177
Sum function 69
Systems unit 10, 14
System tray 16, 51

Online Communication 213
    Webwise 245, 251
    Web Page Creation 189
URL 234
Users 54

Vector file formats 167
Vector images 167
Vector layer 175, 176
    Object selection 178
Vector text 177
Views bar 27
Virus checker 16, 217, 220, 224

Tables 45
    Create 45
    Grid lines 46
Table design
    Database 109, 120
    Word processing 45
Tabs 47
Taskbar 15, 16, 26, 36, 54
Task pane 19, 28
Templates 130
Temporary files 54
Text box 131, 151
Text editor 25
Text entry box 177
Thumbnails 24
Title bar 17
Toolbar 17
Transfer digital photographs 180
Turn off computer 54

Undo 32, 64, 107
Units
    Computing Fundamentals 248
    Create an e-Presentation 147
    Creating Spreadsheets and Graphs 59
    Database Manipulation 101
    e-Image Creation 165
    e-Publication Creation 125
    File Management and e-Document Production 9
    Key Applications 249
    Living Online 250

Webwise Course 251
Web addresses 240
Web page
    Alignment 201
    Background colour 201
    Browser 190, 191
    Build the Web 194
    Check links 204
    Close 198
    Create 199
    Create links 197
    DreamWeaver 190
    Edit hyperlink 205
    Empty Web template 194
    Format 200
    FrontPage 190, 191, 192
        Folders view 192
        HTML view 196
        Hyperlinks view 192, 207
        Navigation view 192
        Normal view 196
        Page view 192
        Preview mode 196, 206
        Reports view 192
    FrontPage themes 201
    Home page 207
    Hosting 191
    HTML 190, 192, 208

HTML Editors 190
Import pages 195
Insert e-mail link 203
Insert image 202
Insert link 203
Insert text 199
Internet Explorer 191
Internet Service Provider 191
Netscape 191
NotePad 191
Open page 196, 198
Preview in Browser 206
Print 208
Publish 191, 209
Publisher 190
Reports 204
Save 198
Standard names 207
Unverified hyperlinks 205
View in browser 206
Web folder 194
Word 190
WYSIWYG 190
XML 190
Your Web 209
Your Web site 193
Web Page Creation 189
Windows Explorer 18
Windows Metafile 167
Windows update 216
Windows XP 12, 19, 127
WordArt
    Presentation graphics 149
Word Count 30
Word processing 25
    Alignment 40
    Backspace 31
    Capitalisation 30
    Delete text 31
    Document standards 30
    Document views 27
    Editing text 31
    File format 25
    Find and replace 43
    Format text 25, 39
    Grammar checking 33
    Margins 27, 29, 30
    Overtype 31
    Page setup 29
    Print document 50
    Print preview 49
    Redo 32
    Ruler 27
    Save
        New file name 34, 35
        New file type 35
        Same file name 35
    Save As 35

Save document 34
Select text 38
Show/hide 31
Spell checking 33
Task pane 27
Toolbars 28
Undo 32
Views bar 27
Zoom level 28
Word vs Publisher 126
Word window 26, 28
Workstation 13
World Wide Web 233
WYSIWYG 25, 190, 196

XML 190
XY line graph 89
X axis 88

Your Web site 193, 209
Y axis 88, 92

Zero point 27
Zoom 28, 49, 173